Executive's
Guide to
Knowledge
Management

Executive's Guide to

KNOWLEDGE MANAGEMENT

THE LAST COMPETITIVE ADVANTAGE

James J. Stapleton

John Wiley & Sons, Inc.

For general information on our other products and services, or technical support, please contact our Customer Care Department within the United States at 800-762-2974, outside the United States at 317-572-3993 or fax 317-572-4002.

Wiley also publishes its books in a variety of electronic formats. Some content that appears in print may not be available in electronic books.

Library of Congress Cataloging-in-Publication Data:
Stapleton, James J.
  Executive's guide to knowledge management : the last competitive advantage / James J. Stapleton.
      p. cm.
Includes index.
   ISBN 0-471-22925-3 (cloth : alk. paper)
  1. Knowledge management.   2. Information resources management.
3. Customer services.   I. Title.
  HD30.2.S782 2003
   658.4'038—dc21

                                                          2002011164

Printed in the United States of America

10 9 8 7 6 5 4 3 2 1

Contents

v

Contents

Contents

Contents

Preface

Some years ago, I had a discussion with a very successful businessman who had decided to retire, though he was in his early fifties. It was a bit surprising, because he had been phenomenally successful in his particular niche, which was turning around failing businesses. To my knowledge, he had few failures, if any, and many successes through the early 1990s. His net worth was well into the nine figures, and his most recent success was fairly impressive, turning around a construction products company that had teetered on the edge of bankruptcy.

COMPETITIVE ADVANTAGES DIMINISHED OR DISAPPEARED

I asked why he was getting out of business at such a comparatively young age, and he replied that it was getting more and more difficult to cut costs and drive revenue.

"Face it," he said. "The traditional areas to gain competitive advantages have disappeared, or are disappearing. It seems as if every area where I've been able to drive value from a business has vanished or shrunk." He pointed out the following:

- ○ Raw materials and inventory
  - The differences in raw material and inventory costs between vendors have shrunk to nearly nothing.
  - Some vendors have gone out of business; many more have been acquired by other concerns. Those that are still independent have to cope with savage price competition.
  - Rival vendors have very little room for error with their own smaller margins.
  - Disintermediation has eliminated layers of manufacturers' representatives, brokers, wholesalers, and other middlemen, squeezing margins further.

- ○ Overhead
  - Metro areas compete to make their business environments as low-cost as possible, in an effort to attract new businesses. Local tax subsidies, rent subsidies, tax credits, low-cost loans, and other incentives drive costs down.
  - Utilities and other related costs are relatively even.
  - The great reengineering expenditures associated with information technology expenditures have come and gone. They have made businesses far more competitive and far more efficient than they ever were.
  - Businesses now compete globally, not locally, so they are competing with very low-cost overseas providers. This hits particularly hard as to labor costs, which are the traditional means of cutting costs.

- ○ Customers
  - Customers are very savvy, and far more cost-conscious than in the past. The incidence of relationships driving purchasing decisions is now rare.
  - Remote purchasing directly through manufacturers or over the Internet has also driven down costs.

○ Profits

- Corporate profits have been squeezed in most businesses.

- Margins in every business have shrunk.

"In short," he summarized, "there's no place left for me to make a profit. I can't cut costs. I can't drive profitable revenue. I can't invent a better mousetrap. So I'm getting out."

This gradual cost and margin compression has resulted in a competitive landscape that places great restraint on margins in businesses in mature or maturing industries. These businesses face dwindling profits, shrinking markets, and encroaching obsolescence.

OBVIOUS WINNERS: INNOVATORS

If you manage to create or invent a solution that solves a vexing business problem, well, you've got it made, providing you can actually bring the solution to market. Obviously, inventiveness and genius are really superior competitive advantages.

THE LAST COMPETITIVE ADVANTAGE

Fresh out of college in 1985, I worked with a small, local accounting firm in Silicon Valley that had few, if any, advantages over other accounting firms in its market. Quite the contrary, it faced many challenges:

○ The accounting profession was mature (even then), and the alumni of the Big Eight dominated the local and regional accounting firm markets.

○ The local firm had no partners who were alumni of the national firms; hence, they had no contacts, no customers, and no referral arrangements with the national firms (unlike their competition).

- The firm was not downtown; it was located in a warehouse district on the outskirts of town, right between an equipment rental store and a machine shop.
- The managing partner began his firm as a 24-year-old with $17,000 in billings in his first year.
- The other two partners had spent just a few years in public accounting. One did not even have an accounting degree and had recently switched careers from private industry.
- All the partners were in their early thirties, and thus did not have the decades-old influencer networks of more senior partners.
- The firm offered no unique services, and the partners' work quality was not dramatically superior to that of other firms.
- The established regional and local accounting firms in the area were founded long before my employer; some had been founded more than a generation earlier.
- The Big Eight firms in Silicon Valley were very hungry and very aggressive with fees. Traditionally, local firms could undercut the costs of the national firms, but in Silicon Valley, the national firms typically bid a fraction of what local firms would charge because of the tremendous upside potential of Silicon Valley concerns.

The average annual growth rate of a local accounting firm at the time was about 6 percent. At the time, the firm grossed about $250,000 per partner, with net income averaging about $100,000 per partner. Ten years later, the firm grew from 3 partners to 17. Average billings per partner were approaching $1 million. What happened?

The chief advantage that firm had over its competition (350 firms and practitioners in the geographic market) was a knowledge-generating apparatus that was second to none and light-years ahead of its time. The firm had near-perfect knowledge on its customers, its contacts and leads, the industries it served, the competition, the local movers and shakers, and the dynamics of the local economy. This company used its knowledge filters to great advantage in building an exceptional knowledge base. At any given time:

- It knew when all its contacts and leads were on the brink of switching firms.
- It had profiles on every prospective customer in its market.
- It had complete summaries on the strengths, weaknesses, market approaches, and predilections of their competition.
- It had relationship maps between all appropriate influencers and the competition.
- It had many, many other information advantages over its competitors.

Rarely did clients, prospects, influencer networks, or industry contacts surprise this firm's staff. When those infrequent occasions occurred, the firm thoroughly examined the situation from all angles, distributed the information to every partner (sometimes every employee), and worked overtime to fix the situation.

In summary, most companies are woefully ignorant of the dynamics surrounding their businesses. A comprehensive effort at building knowledge can only aid in their efforts.

WHAT THIS BOOK IS ABOUT

Superficially, this book is about improving the efficiency of the gathering, evaluation, organization, analysis, dissemination, and employment of information and production of knowledge by decision makers in small- to mid-sized businesses. However, this book is *really* about other things.

In my opinion, the single greatest business challenge of the twentieth century lay in acquiring information and data. In the twenty-first century, that challenge inheres in fulfilling two goals:

1. Ensuring that all individuals in an enterprise have appropriate access to knowledge and the ability to act on it in the way most meaningful to the enterprise. To that end, we will examine the intermediate steps that surround the knowledge-generating process, the weaknesses inherent in the standard course of action, and how to improve your procedures to create the maximum benefit.

2. We will concentrate on determining and defining many of the subjective factors in the information-gathering process. This is where the typical business suffers a breakdown.

Ultimately, the goal of this book is to enable you to apply a coordinated approach for realizing the vast knowledge potential inherent in your business.

THE CHALLENGE

There has always been a need for answers; for reliable information and data; and for high-quality, objective, forward-looking research and analysis, across all industries. The key challenge is to identify and isolate the appropriate inputs and synthesize them into applicable knowledge.

The need comes from executives who must understand and navigate through increasingly demanding market conditions (technological change, globalization, deregulation, and other disruptive changes) that bring new opportunities, new competitors, and new risks. In this environment, the right answers, information, and analysis provide a firm foundation for managerial decision making. Information gathering and synthesis also provide the planning process, integrity, and credibility sought by shareholders, directors, customers, suppliers, and analysts.

This applies not just to large corporations with substantial in-house research staff and the resources to undertake or purchase customized research. The business needs are every bit as compelling for smaller firms, which typically lie below the radar screen of major competitors.

Our premise is that sophisticated global competition has made it increasingly difficult to achieve a significant material advantage over one's competition based on either cost reduction or revenue maximization. Currently, most businesses must satisfy themselves with razor-thin improvements over their cost structures. There are few, if any, substantial gains to be accrued through cost reduction. Producer margins, overhead, labor, inventory, and other cost burdens have all been trimmed to the bone through years of advancements, low-cost rivals (overseas and otherwise), disintermediation, e-business, enterprise resource planning (ERP) implementation, and other factors.

Conversely, it is expensive to add incremental revenue. Customers demand lenient conditions, extended payment terms, expensive support, and six-sigma quality. Discounting has become more and more prevalent. Long-time relationships mean less as customers seek to cut costs. Sales forces, brokers, and sales representatives are expensive and further reduce margins. Nontraditional, low-cost sales channels have difficulty gaining attention and mind share.

THE *ONLY* BUSINESS BATTLEFIELD

The only business battlefield that can really be taken lies between the ears. To beat the competition, management must be smarter, craftier, and more cunning. Management usually understands this instinctively, and this tends to point toward securing additional information. There is no dearth of information, what with the explosion of information available on the Internet, from trade and industry organizations and associations, from information cooperatives, in benchmarking databases, and through professional researchers and research organizations such as Forrester Research, IDC, and Gartner.

POST-INFORMATION ECONOMY

Because of the information explosion, information (in and of itself) has become as much a commodity as anything else: cheap and widely available, bordering on generic. Applicable knowledge, appropriately utilized, is the key to success.

The success or failure of a business lies in a series, a sequence of decisions. Each decision made by an executive or business owner is based on that person's existing knowledge. These decisions, from the momentary to the momentous, rest on the foundation of knowledge supported by a myriad of inputs.

This book has two primary purposes. First, it reviews the steps of turning information into knowledge useful enough to improve your business. Outwardly, the steps appear simple. In reality, each step is fraught with potential for mismanagement. Second, it presents the experience and wisdom developed by the author in nearly 20 years as an information professional.

How important is it to have a sophisticated information-generating mechanism? Realistically, how much of a difference can it make?

Knowledge management appeals to all working adults, because all working adults operate in the knowledge economy. No one is exempt. Everyone must use information, whether they are evaluating internal or external dynamic information flows. A few years back, Silicon Valley Bank interviewed its business customers and asked them to rank the importance of 17 different measurable factors. By far, the most important category was "information, data, knowledge and research." Readers will purchase this book because they realize that the single remaining true competitive advantage they have left over their competition is applied knowledge. Labor is nearly fixed, materials costs are fixed, all but the top-end manufacturing is offshore, rent and other utilities are common-cost burdens. All these areas have historically offered competitive advantages. Today, however, the advantages of each have been flattened out through a century of national and international competition.

One competitive factor remains: applied knowledge. When all else is equal, information, data, and knowledge drive the market and the success of the companies in it.

10 STEPS TO TURNING INFORMATION INTO KNOWLEDGE

Transforming information into knowledge requires 10 discrete steps. Each has to be carefully managed. Most are deceptively complex and can easily lead one astray. It is important to note that one's knowledge is only as strong as the weakest of these 10 steps.

1. *Find it.* Anyone who has conducted an Internet search knows that there are hundreds, if not thousands, of sources for a piece of information. It is one of the most difficult components of creating knowledge. Where will your base data come from?

2. *Get it.* Particularly with a customized search for information, it is critical that information be secured in the original and that the compiler be a trusted source. Always question the source. Get all the information, not just select information.

3. *Evaluate it.* Every bit of information has to be evaluated, in terms of quality, context, and age (information has the shelf life of milk), in respect to other compiled information. Again, consider the source. I know of two industry surveys: one compiled by a wealthy statistician, one compiled by a not-so-wealthy marketer. Interestingly, the marketer compiles the accurate survey. The statistician, for a broad variety of reasons, compiles an exceedingly inaccurate survey. Does the information pass the smell test?

4. *Compile it.* Transcribe it properly. Information can come in different shades. This is no joke—accuracy is critical. For example, a nationally syndicated reporter once compiled information on saving the Social Security trust fund.

She reported that a mere 2 percent increase in the Social Security withholding tax would be sufficient to save the fund. There was just one slight problem: due to her compilation error, she was off by a factor of 15. In other words, the Social Security withholding tax would have had to increase by 30 percent to save the fund. The error undermined her entire article.

5. *Understand it.* Information doesn't come with directions. It has different meanings to different people. Everyone has a different perspective, everyone has different goals, everyone has different agendas, everyone has different backgrounds. It all shapes one's understanding of the information.

6. *Analyze it.* To go one step beyond understanding the data, one has to evaluate information in light of all other factors: common knowledge, industry standards, relationships, tendencies to change, and so on.

7. *Synthesize it.* Information has to be consolidated. A salesman may get a hundred pages of information and need to reduce it to one page of bullet points. Which are the right bullet points?

8. *Disseminate/distribute it.* Information has to get to the right people. This is a huge problem in business and is possibly the most problematic of these 10 steps. An entire book could be written about this issue, much of it centered on interpersonal relationships. Information, particularly customized information, can be highly valued inside an organization; hence, it can be protected, traded, stifled, hidden, embellished, or spun.

9. *Act on it.* A warehouse of books has been written on the importance of making decisions and volumes have been written on using information, data, and knowledge in those decisions. What makes a decision well informed?

10. *Combine it. Maintain it. Update it.* Information is living, dynamic. It has to be banked, managed, maintained, and

continually updated. It has to be leavened with other data and opinions. It has to be refreshed; old data has to be pruned from it (excepting trend analysis). Only then does it become knowledge. Information gets stale. Knowledge gains in strength.

THE MASTER'S COURSE

Once the reader has mastered these basic steps, we give the reader a master's course in turning information into knowledge, by delving into some of the methods, experiences, and drawbacks uncovered during the author's 20 years as an information specialist.

WHAT THIS BOOK IS NOT ABOUT

- It is not about innovation, genius, or invention. That is a different kind of competitive advantage.
- It is not about delivering information through ERP systems, nor is it about information technology or data storage. There are many fine books on data storage, data retrieval, data mining, and the various ways to slice and cut data. You will not find that discussion here.
- It is not a treatise on empirical information. The real world is messy and disturbing. Information always gets filtered through the prism of opinion, preconceptions, and perspectives.
- It is not about the post-information economy. That is an enormous topic. It is much simpler for authors to deal with narrower topics, so we have tried to do that here.
- It is not focused on very large companies or industry-specific portions of the market.
- It is not an academic treatise. We are trying to stay accessible to everyone.

INFOSHOCK

The only term to use for the state businesses will reach is *infoshock*—a state of shock. Shock at how little control they have over the factors that previously determined their success or failure. Shock over their inability to control costs or drive profitable revenue. Shock at the nature of successful emerging businesses. The deepest shock will probably be reserved for how much better their companies could and must be at managing the myriad of data, opinion, and information inputs to improve their business.

To prepare yourself for infoshock, we first examine the *info-mentality*, the state of mind developed for best organizing an array of inputs into usable, applicable knowledge. It is truly the only competitive advantage remaining. Here is how you can use it to destroy your competition.

1

Infomentality

Insofar as a business is concerned, intelligence gathering is so important and permeates so many aspects of the business, it is indistinguishable from the business itself.

In this book, *intelligence gathering* is defined as the process of securing the secret or uncovered information, data, opinions, and knowledge on markets, competitors, prospects, influencers, and clients in order to satisfy organizational objectives. Intelligence gathering is indeed a process, not a project, and all tactical intelligence-gathering activities are mere functions of your overall intelligence-gathering strategy. Intelligence gathering is a comprehensive, long-term, balanced approach that encompasses developing new skills; testing effective communication techniques; identifying information, knowledge, opinion, and data needs; and setting proper pricing policies. These activities can be coordinated into an effective intelligence-gathering strategy.

Businesspersons must adopt the attitude that *every bit* of information, data, and opinion they gather affects the knowledge base of their business. The flow of intelligence, whether private or public, is in constant motion, and it is surprisingly easy to access it to direct your corporate strategies.

YOUR INFOMENTALITY

Because of the combination of factors that create rising costs, shrinking markets, and burgeoning competition, intelligence gathering is no longer treated as a dirty word. Intelligence gathering is an essential function, not only in terms of expanding market share in traditional areas, but also in terms of protecting existing market share from aggressive competitors. Intelligence gathering is more than just general business knowledge: It directly enhances your ability to meet clients' needs and solve their problems.

INTELLIGENCE-GATHERING MENTALITY

Everyone in business is at least subconsciously aware of the need to gather information. An intelligence-gathering mentality means gearing your mind to be aware of all opportunities for knowledge building, and to be aware that everything you do, no matter how mundane, has the potential to affect a customer or a contact. A successful businessperson sells every day by rendering quality service and by treating her surrounding community of contacts accordingly. A successful businessperson understands the concept of the competitive market. She realizes that:

- ○ Intelligence gathering enables you to grow with your customers and keep them satisfied.
- ○ It is important to keep your customers satisfied—better yet, ecstatic—because your competition is not quitting tomorrow.
- ○ An intelligence-gathering mentality, as well as an information-gathering program, gives you a significant advantage over competitors who have stopped gathering information.

○ An intelligence-gathering program is important to an established business because the market is dynamic. It is constantly changing. Competitors come and go, businesses are established and businesses fail.

○ Your positive reputation will be the only thing to sustain your business in lean times. Your reputation brings in customers and, just as important, keeps old customers from leaving. It keeps information sources impressed with your quality, and keeps the movers and shakers in your corner.

○ It is important to have these people behind you because people forget fast. A business is on top one day, and an also-ran the next.

○ Though you may feel your knowledge management is acceptable, you must pay attention to the program, because intelligence gathering improves the morale of your employees.

○ Employees with high morale cement relations with your customers.

○ Your intelligence-gathering successes are inseparable from the service itself, which means you should take pains to educate the customer. Intelligence gathering is a process of education, not selling.

Part of an intelligence-gathering mentality is acknowledging that certain market forces hold sway. You must acknowledge the following as business reality:

○ *Market share matters.* There is absolutely no need for you to be satisfied with the size and composition of your business. I once saw the financial statement of a very successful local real estate business, in which each broker was making more than $300,000 annually. Still, the chief executive officer (CEO) wanted to grow. He stated, "I can't be satisfied until I'm certain that we are doing all we can to make our business the best it can be. Anything less is a half-hearted effort and is unacceptable."

○ *There is no substitute for quality.* If your business is the seed, quality is the soil. Mediocre quality breeds a mediocre business. Improve the quality of your work on a regular basis. If you have not already had one, consider an external knowledge management review to see (1) how your firm is perceiving the market, and (2) how closely your self-image matches those perceptions.

○ *People make a difference.* Perhaps one of the most difficult tasks for a consultant is working with moribund businesses whose owners decide, out of the blue, that the time is right for growth and engage the consultant to work a miracle. Your people form the foundation of your intelligence-gathering effort because of their effect on your quality level. Your intelligence-gathering success is limited by the intelligence-gathering aptitude of your people. If you have staffers who have never gathered intelligence in any capacity, nor demonstrated any aptitude for it, you are facing a long uphill struggle.

One of my customers stated point blank that the most difficult thing he had to do to achieve intelligence-gathering success was to turn the responsibility over to his staff. He began with a five-year plan, and at the end of five years, 90 percent of his staff was gone—only the smart people were left.

○ *If it ain't broke, fix it anyway.* All the best companies attack themselves by reinventing or improving on their products. You can do the same thing with your competitor intelligence program. Such programs tend to require continuous updating.

Desire

Winning isn't everything. The desire to win is everything. In fact, it's the only thing.

—Vince Lombardi (what he *really* said)

Desire is at the base of the intelligence-gathering mentality. The intensity of your intelligence-gathering mentality rests on your desire to grow, or to improve your business to the point where it is operating at peak efficiency. It is not enough to be ready to grow; you must *want* to grow, and believe you can engage that large customer, or service a customer twice as big as your largest current customer.

This section is not intended to be a pep talk; frankly, if your motivation comes from external sources, you are not ready for a concentrated intelligence-gathering program. If you do not believe that you are ready to secure a customer that is larger than your largest customer, your intelligence-gathering program will sputter and fail. But if you have the confidence to succeed and gain market share, you will do so.

One of the most debilitating and, unfortunately, most common problems today is the businessperson who pays lip service to intelligence gathering for the business. The sad thing is that it does not have to happen. Let's examine why many managers lack the special, inborn desire to market and/or grow.

A senior manager enjoys a unique kind of security almost like tenure at a university. Only after a particularly heinous mistake, or series of mistakes, does a company even consider asking a manager to leave. Managers enjoy security and high rates of financial return, and personal bankruptcy is virtually unknown. Customers' psychological and emotional commitment to managers and vendors is fairly high; if a customer is extended even minimally acceptable service, it is unlikely to leave. Therefore, loss of business is rarely a problem, and thus managers are assured security.

When senior managers become too secure, however, they can become insensitive to change in the marketplace. They lose the instincts that got them to their current positions. The first sign is their failure to gather and use information.

Another reason many businesses become stagnant is that most businesspersons are technically oriented and comparatively unfamiliar with intelligence-gathering goals or methods. They define intelligence gathering in its narrowest sense. They halfheartedly participate in a few seminars, throw a little time and money at the intelligence-gathering issue, and then conclude that their intelligence-gathering effort did nothing to improve their reputation or customer base. They shrug their shoulders, fully believing that they extended themselves to the intelligence-gathering limit, and go back to worrying about which of their customers will be shopping vendors next.

Businesses often exacerbate this problem from the beginning of a young manager's career. An employee sees promotion up the ladder as a sort of golden carrot, a goal to pursue mercilessly. A senior manager sits on a lofty, rarefied perch that is perceived by subordinate employees as a kind of business nirvana. Once an employee becomes a manager, there is a danger that he or she will treat it almost as tenure and slack off because he or she has "made it."

Without desire, an intelligence-gathering mentality cannot be formed and an intelligence-gathering program is doomed to failure. To understand desire, or lack thereof, you must understand your motivation.

Motivation

Enthusiasm is one of the most powerful engines of success. When you do a thing, do it with all your might. Put your whole soul into it. Stamp it with your own personality. Be active, be energetic, and enthusiastic, and you will accomplish your objective. Nothing great was ever achieved without enthusiasm.

—Teddy Roosevelt

There are businesspersons who are driven to secure good business and careful to keep it from slipping out the back door. There are businesspersons who are good technical people but are tentative in intelligence-gathering situations. And there are certainly managers who pay lip service to intelligence gathering in managerial meetings, but lack the interest or time, or both, to become good knowledge warriors. Nowadays, if someone has difficulty drumming up business, it is almost impossible for him or her to get promoted to the senior ranks. It is common for large businesses to release managers who do not bring in business.

Why do aggressive businesses and aggressive managers bring in such a large quantity of business? Why do they seem to perform at high levels? There are several reasons:

- People admire companies that openly cultivate new business. Customers assume that they will receive better service and be treated better than by aloof businesses. Not surprisingly, aggressive businesses usually have enough capacity to accept new customers and perform well for them.

- These businesses perform excellent followup. They pay attention to detail.

- Aggressive businesses *ask* for business. This sounds simple, but it is key. Many managers expect the business from a potential lead but do not ask for it. Several of these indifferent managers have said, "Ask for it? Why do I need to ask for it? They know I want it!" All customers know is that a businessperson who asks for the business wants it too, and the actual asking demonstrates it.

- Aggressive businesses market additional services to their current customers. When current customers make greater use of your business, they are more loyal, because they have a stronger relationship. The insurance industry has recognized this for years, which is why they want you to purchase not only auto insurance from their business, but home, life, medical, and umbrella coverage as well. One insurance agent said that if he sells one policy to a customer, there is only a 10 percent chance that he will have that customer 10 years down the road. But if he sells 2 policies to the customer, there is a 60 percent chance that the customer will still be a customer in 10 years; and if he sells 3 or more policies to a customer, there is a 95 percent chance that the customer will still be with him in 10 years.

o Aggressive businesses are more accessible to customers.

o Aggressive businesses always tell customers how much they appreciate their business.

Building New Business

These reasons highlight the revenue-generating benefits of aggressive managers. The same methods and personalities work as aggressive intelligence-gathering postures.

Consider, for example, the life of a senior manager. He has a large income, and a beautiful home with enough material possessions to be quite happy. He has a happy family that he rarely sees (in fact, sometimes he is just a rumor). The manager has a good future in a business with unspectacular but steady growth. With all this going for him, why would he need more information? Why does he need the headaches of more intelligence, or the additional headaches of searching for this intelligence?

Some managers are naturally hungry. These are the managers who love to grow for growth's sake, who never have enough business. They have the material things, but they want more: emotional satisfaction from their growing business, a desire for more money, a need for new customers and prestige. Obviously, there are many different psychological and emotional reasons why some managers want to grow, whereas others merely want to maintain the status quo. As part of this personality makeup, they have a desire, a motivation to gather intelligence and information to further their growth goals.

The single most difficult thing managers normally face is disagreements with their peers, their fellow managers. If a clerical person or staffer clashes with established business policy, it is not too difficult to convince him or her that a mutual parting is for the best. But because a manager is such an intricate part of the business, a mere lack of a "hungry" attitude is ordinarily not enough to doom that manager. We are all aware, however, of situations in which this lack of desire *was* sufficient to require the manager's resignation.

ELEMENTS OF THE INTELLIGENCE-GATHERING MENTALITY

Seven basic elements are required to establish a intelligence-gathering mentality:

1. Desire
2. Commitment
3. Followup
4. Unity of effort
5. Communication
6. Intelligence-gathering activities
7. Acceptance of change

Desire

Before commitment, there must be interest. Everyone knows people who refuse to participate in any intelligence-gathering activity—who feel that aggressive intelligence-gathering techniques are wrong. Also common are businesspersons who exert a minimum of time and energy on intelligence-gathering tasks. These are the managers who are surprised by the lack of return their intelligence-gathering effort brings.

Desire for new business is the cornerstone of your intelligence-gathering effort. To cultivate desire is to cultivate the desired results. Some managers focus on intelligence gathering as their primary activity. All of these managers are successful at acquiring new business, and not all of them have sales personalities. In fact, a sales personality is unnecessary for a successful intelligence-gathering effort.

The strongest, most fundamental element of a intelligence-gathering mentality is desire. Your level of desire foreshadows your level of results.

Commitment

Perhaps the most frustrating thing for a businessperson is to work with someone who lacks regard or concern for a thriving business. The first theorem of commitment is: Unless all managers are committed to intelligence gathering, you are lost.

Like many businesses, one particular business had a superstar CEO. Somehow, some way, he managed to generate more information than anyone in the industry. Although his intelligence-gathering skills certainly ensured his own personal success, a far more important (and much rarer) skill was his ability to transfer his information-gathering skills to his managers and staff. He constantly shared his philosophy and experiences with his managers to demonstrate his own commitment to servicing customers and developing new business. His commitment supported the commitment of his managers and staff.

For example, one of his managers was a thoroughly competent practitioner who had not previously been required to gather information. With the CEO's consistent encouragement, assistance, and supervision, the manager evolved his natural tenacity into superb followup and developed an enviable database of intelligence sources.

Apart from desire, the most critical factor in an intelligence-gathering mentality is the managers' commitment to intelligence gathering. This is a fundamental component of your business's intelligence-gathering effort. Ask yourself: Is your business committed to intelligence gathering? Are your managers? Is it a team effort?

Some people initially want to develop business and perform all of the intelligence-gathering activities that will make their practices grow. However, one must understand what a vast amount of

10

energy a consistent intelligence-gathering effort consumes. It is easy to lose interest when one discovers that growth does not come easily, or all at once. Managers who want to grow must be aware that commitment is a prerequisite for growth.

Follow-up

Even the most diligent, intelligence-aware manager gets behind at times. In fact, the best managers lag somewhat behind simply because of the immense amount of information they generate. Consequently, there is a danger of contacts, leads, and even new customers slipping through the cracks—if the cracks become wide enough.

There must be a designated person or program to follow up on *all* new intelligence, data, and applicable knowledge. Of course, it is best if you pursue your own contacts and perform followup functions yourself. You are familiar with the contact or the customer, and this builds trust and consistency. You may be overloaded, however, so one individual should be designated an intelligence-gathering watchdog. This person is responsible for maintaining a list of contacts and a followup schedule, and should remind everyone of followup calls, letters, and other activities. Only if you do not have the time should someone else place the first followup call.

A manager is not necessarily an effective watchdog. Watchdog activities hinder a manager's individual intelligence-gathering efforts. If you must keep on top of your managers, not only are you removed from your other activities, but your managers are also demonstrating a lack of desire. Again, without desire, commitment, and followup, your intelligence-gathering effort is doomed from the beginning.

Unity of Effort

A business needs a common direction; first and foremost, you need to know where you are going. You should set goals and follow them (explained in detail in this chapter, under "Your Intelligence-Gathering Plan"). Whatever you call it—vision, direction, goals—you need a strategic plan to rally around. Not only does it provide guidance, but it also functions as an automatic means of auditing the intelligence-gathering program.

The worst mistake a CEO can make is to present an intelligence-gathering program by fiat to her managers. It is worse than no program at all, because it wastes business resources and is not based on common goals or common directions. Your managers may smile and agree outwardly, but if they feel they have no choice but to accept it, they will rebel. Therefore, a CEO must ask both herself and her managers what direction the *business* wants to take. The perceptions and attitudes of the senior people in the business will be the foundation for the business's positioning and intelligence-gathering strategy, and will form the critical infrastructure. If the managers are pulling the business in different directions, the business may stagnate, but if the managers move in a common direction, the business will succeed. A united effort is essential to intelligence-gathering success.

There is a business that has experienced explosive success during the past half-dozen years, outdistancing its nearest competitor's growth threefold. One of the secrets is that the CEO of this business has a vision, and he ensures that everyone remains true to the vision.

After several years of rapid growth, the CEO felt that a more cohesive plan was required. Like all businesses, they held regularly scheduled manager meetings. These meetings were primarily tactical in nature; rarely did they explicitly discuss business strategy. The business strategy and direction, however, were implicit in the decisions and resolution of issues during the meetings.

One day, the CEO gathered together all the managers and senior personnel, not to present them with a statement of the business's direction, but to canvass the people whose everyday work and decisions had an impact on the future of the business.

He asked all of the attendees to take several minutes to answer (anonymously) the following two questions:

1. Where do I see the business's progress in terms of number of offices, managers, departments, specialties, number of employees, and structure in two years? In five years? In ten years?
2. How do I perceive my progress and my contribution to the business over the next two years? Over the next five years? During the next ten years?

With this simple exercise, he revealed the motivations, expectations, and goals of his key personnel. By revealing the states of mind of his key personnel, he could gauge their motivations, the depth of their commitment, and the consistency of their goals with his vision.

What else has the CEO uncovered? From the motivations, expectations, and goals of his personnel, he can extrapolate several things:

○ The level of effort each person was willing to contribute.
○ Their thought processes and mindsets as they would affect the business and the vision of the CEO.
○ Cohesiveness among the managers.
○ Level of satisfaction with the progress of the business.
○ Willingness of the participants to contribute to the CEO's vision.
○ Level of intelligence-gathering mentality that each participant displayed.

Communication

The manager should initiate all communication between himself and the contact. The only exception to this rule is when it is obviously beneficial for another person to be brought into play.

This is much rarer than one might think. A contact is nervous;

by giving you information, she is taking a leap of faith that portends marginal good for what could potentially be disastrously bad. The contact needs to be calmed constantly until she is certain that she has made the best strategic move.

Intelligence-Gathering Activities

A business must fully realize the extent of the changes in the marketplace if it is to develop a successful intelligence-gathering program. After the managers have unified their efforts, the success of the program will depend upon the effect of the intelligence-gathering activities. Creating an aggressive intelligence-gathering program involves more than just spending money on industry experts, researchers, analysts, and so on; it means changing the fundamental structure of the business to become more profitable, to free up more intelligence-gathering time for the managers, to inculcate an intelligence-gathering mentality, and to communicate goals, strategies, and responsibilities.

Acceptance of Change

By accepting change in the fundamental structure of your business, your managers lay the foundation for growth. Everyone in your business needs to be aware of your new intelligence-gathering mentality and commitment. Keep in mind that resistance to change by your staff is your greatest challenge, so focus your energies to counter any resistance very early on.

YOUR INTELLIGENCE-GATHERING PLAN

Intelligence gathering is a dynamic, constantly changing process. The intelligence factors surrounding your business are in a constant state of flux, insidious in that they sneak up on you and change the rules of the game. This is true not only of the market forces directly affecting you, but also of the overlapping factors that touch upon your services.

Designing, implementing, and updating your intelligence-gathering plan is so critical that a separate chapter is devoted entirely to producing a successful intelligence-gathering plan (see Chapter 8). It details the 10 elements required for your intelligence-gathering plan:

1. Understanding the gathering process
2. Using all available resources
3. Training everyone in gathering intelligence
4. Finding information on the marketplace
5. Getting and maintaining excellent rapport with customers
6. Building solid infrastructure and total staff involvement
7. Fostering intelligence-gathering ability
8. Growing sales ability
9. Projecting a positive business image
10. Investing extra time and effort

Understanding the Gathering Process

All successful businesspeople constantly reevaluate the markets, their positions, their pricing, and their services. Remember that intelligence gathering is neither stagnant nor a mere data retrieval process (though data retrieval will be an aspect of your intelligence-gathering plan). Intelligence gathering is an ongoing process, formed by an awareness of the current market environment, your professional information sources, your customers, your prospects, your influencers, industry and media sources, your competition, your partners, and your staff.

Using All Available Resources

Your intelligence-gathering program must be unique, maximizing the talents of you, your business, and all available resources. It will require a realistic approach to match your internal resources, external capabilities, and the aptitude of your people. Use your own talents and your entire staff's talents to the fullest, but do not attempt activities that are inappropriate for your business.

Athletes talk about "playing within themselves," and this holds true as well for internal intelligence-gathering efforts. Typically, though, not all answers are found inside your organization. External resources are needed to round out your efforts.

Training Everyone in Gathering Intelligence

Businesses that jump into an intelligence-gathering program without really understanding the strategies, tools, ramifications, and results of each intelligence-gathering activity are just asking for problems. It is almost guaranteed that these businesses will be disappointed with their results, because they will be acting merely from preconceived notions, rather than actual knowledge and understanding of the underlying reasons for and benefits of each activity.

When educating your staff, ensure that each person has an intelligence-gathering mentality. They need to understand what type of information contributes to the business's knowledge base and they need to understand that information can be found everywhere.

Finding Information in the Marketplace

Information finding is an area that remains largely closed to businesses by virtue of the secretive nature of the profession. However, there are ways to obtain information, and you should use all the resources available to establish databases of information on customers, contacts, information sources, and your competition. After establishing your information on the marketplace in a database, keep it current. As previously mentioned, the market is constantly changing, so you must keep your database updated.

Getting and Maintaining Excellent Rapport with Current Customers

A customer-oriented business has a huge head start on a task-oriented or a technically oriented business in terms of gathering information. A customer-oriented business actively manages and controls communication with its customers. Through excellent rapport with your customers, you will create a comfort level that effectively shields you from competitors, and provides an atmosphere more conducive to gathering referrals and selling additional services. Also, your public image is invariably positive with this kind of rapport. As the old saying goes, alienate your customers, and you won't need any enemies.

Building Solid Infrastructure and Total Staff Involvement

There was a business in my area that had an astounding growth rate. For the first five years of its existence, the business doubled in size every year. During the next six years, the business doubled in size every other year, until it was finally bought out by a national concern. Out of curiosity, I asked the business's former intelligence-gathering director why they seemed to be on top of the market much more successfully than others. She replied that the business did just two things to achieve success: first, they kept their eyes open for every potential information source that became available for purchase or merger; second, every employee was required to evaluate the information environment on a weekly basis. This meant that the employees had to get to know their markets, their competition, their clients, and their prospects. In other words, they had to act as if they were management.

Does this sound extreme? When you consider how much time is available in a week and how much is really required for success, it was not so difficult. What really made it work was the involvement of the managers and staffers.

Your best strategy is to agree on a documented intelligence-gathering policy with your management and employees. When the business's intelligence-gathering policy is in writing, there will be no questions about the business's intelligence-gathering direction, and you can move forward in that clear direction. Clarity allows change to occur more smoothly—crucial for any dynamic business environment.

Your intelligence-gathering program infrastructure, heretofore referred to as the *intelligence-gathering plan,* is the basis of your business's intelligence-gathering mentality. A truly successful intelligence-gathering program *always* involves everyone in the business. The more staff you involve in your intelligence-gathering program, the better chance you have at growing successfully. Your employees should be optimistic, enthusiastic, and zealous. Commitment and active participation of the entire staff are two of the few intelligence-gathering activities that will really cause the business to succeed. Unfortunately, this is one of the most neglected areas of intelligence gathering for businesses.

Remember, everyone connected with the business gathers intelligence.

Fostering Intelligence-Gathering Ability

Every business concern needs some form of intelligence gathering, some information development arm. The underlying assumption is that every business needs effective intelligence-gathering methods that uncover customers who are either unhappy with their current vendor, or are not receiving the service to which they are entitled; or reveal competitor strategies; or highlight future industry problems; or turn up a myriad of other interesting items.

Most businesspersons take a narrow view of intelligence gathering. This attitude actually makes it easier to be successful.

18

Growing Sales Ability

Many businesspersons would prefer to leave sales to salespersons. They feel that sales might demean whatever it is that they do. They equate sales with annoying, high-pressure, foot-in-the-door tactics.

The fact of the matter is that gathering information can be an aggressive act, particularly when you are gathering it directly from individual contacts. You do need to sell to your contacts—but before you cringe at the thought, understand it in its most positive sense. This does not refer to high-pressure tactics or trickery.

You offer a product or service. Demanding customers, concerned influencers, and skeptical prospects will all do business with the company that best conveys its strengths. This business comes through one-on-one interpersonal skills. Remember, though, that *interpersonal skill* does not merely mean selling. Selling is just face-to-face intelligence gathering.

You are involved in sales every day. Every contact you have with each customer, referral source, or potential customer demonstrates the innate qualities you have that will keep these people associating with you. The lack of this ability, this interpersonal skill, would result in a diminished image and professional reputation, a loss of customers, and ultimately a loss of market information.

Every businessperson has reached a certain level of sales ability, and these skills are generally augmented by continuous customer contact. However, few businesspersons are expert salespersons, and almost all businesspersons could stand to improve their skills. It does not matter how many contacts you secure, but how many customers you engage.

Projecting a Positive Business Image

Obviously, a negative image is out of the question! But even a neutral image is unacceptable, as it can actually harm your intelligence-gathering program. Neutrality is static; it creates no impetus for change.

Many parts of a intelligence-gathering plan amount to planting seeds. A public relations program is one of them. The business's image and reputation are important, not only for intelligence-gathering success, but because recognition positively motivates staff, information sources, customers, and contacts.

Investing Extra Time and Effort

You must carve out time to build knowledge. When I was a junior operations officer, our CEO, Dave, strolled into our war room deep in thought. This caused us all to sit up and take notice. There were 9 of us at the startup and we were young, aggressive, and energetic, working 16-hour days and rarely taking the time to catch our breath. In particular, Dave was manic. This was perhaps the first time we had ever seen him in a thoughtful mode.

He explained that he had been at his monthly Executive Committee meeting, which was his chance to interface with other CEOs. Once a month, he would gather with 20 of his peers to discuss issues, problems, ideas, and other concerns that can really be aired or resolved only at the CEO level. After their conversations, they had a speaker. On that particular day, the speaker was an ex-Army Chief of Intelligence who had set up shop as a business intelligence consultant. We thought it odd that Dave was reflective after the meeting—actually, it was a state of controlled panic.

He said, "Let me ask you all a question." He looked around the room. "What do we know about our competitors? Our vendors? Our manufacturer's reps? Our business environment?" We all threw in some items . . . clearly, none of us was as knowledgeable as we should have been. Dave said, "I want each of us to spend four hours per week *minimum* on learning. I want to know the competition, the status of patents, what the customers think, what the vendors think, what our reps are saying. I want each of you to cultivate a relationship with one media outlet and one analyst." He continued, assigning tasks to each of us. That day, we created the means to sharpen our sword.

The final component of the intelligence-gathering mentality is time and effort. If you do comparatively little intelligence gathering now, and are completely fatigued at the end of the day, you do not have the energy for a sustained, concentrated intelligence-gathering effort. Further, if your customer load is so heavy that you wonder how you can take on any more business, you need to become more efficient, build more production, or hire more staff. Again, a choice is required. You must either trim the unprofitable customers from your customer list, or add customers to support your infrastructure.

FEAR ACCEPTED WISDOM

At its base, the gathering of intelligence causes you to question accepted wisdom. That's good—nothing can be more damaging than the accepted wisdom! It leads to flabby strategies, poor execution, avoidance of challenges, and surprises from the competition. Your intelligence-gathering program should cause you to view accepted wisdom with a jaundiced eye.

THE TRAP OF MUNDANE TASKS

We are all racing to keep up at the breakneck pace of business. No one is immune. The race for efficiency over the last 25 years has stripped us of much of our ability to free-think, to examine our environment, to generate knowledge. The multiple pursuits of signing customers and keeping them happy, gathering better products and services, holding costs down, and other challenges have left us with precious little time to take an aggressive approach to learning about our environments.

CONCLUSION

In this chapter, we discussed the changes you must make within your business to prepare for an intelligence-gathering plan. Creating a successful, aggressive intelligence-gathering plan requires a fundamental change at the heart of a business's structure, goals, and philosophy (assuming the business is not currently market-aware or oriented to intelligence gathering). Is your support structure conducive to the intelligence-gathering task? Can you effectively disseminate the information? Do you trust your employees with the information? Are they motivated enough to seek additional information? Do they have the time, technical expertise, and organizational skills to get the information? Your fundamental structure must encompass a total approach to intelligence gathering.

Most importantly, do you, your managers, and your business have an intelligence-gathering mentality? The intelligence-gathering mentality is the key to success for all businesses, no matter what size. The intelligence-gathering mentality is the foundation from which to derive successful growth.

2

InfoGoals

Real knowledge is to know the extent of one's ignorance.
—Confucius

What are the goals of a knowledge development program? Simply put, the goal of producing information is to develop and manage applicable knowledge that is useful for making business decisions (see Exhibit 2.1). There are three key subgoals:

1. Turn the disparate opinions, information, and data into usable business knowledge.
2. Act on this knowledge to bolster the strategies and tactics employed by the business.
3. Maintain and update the accumulated knowledge on a regular basis.

As it is for individuals, so it is for businesses. Learn, transfer it to real-world knowledge, and grow.

SIMPLE INFORMATION REQUEST

An apparently straightforward search for information is rarely uncomplicated. Here's a true story. The manager in charge of a

Exhibit 2.1   Building Knowledge Flowchart

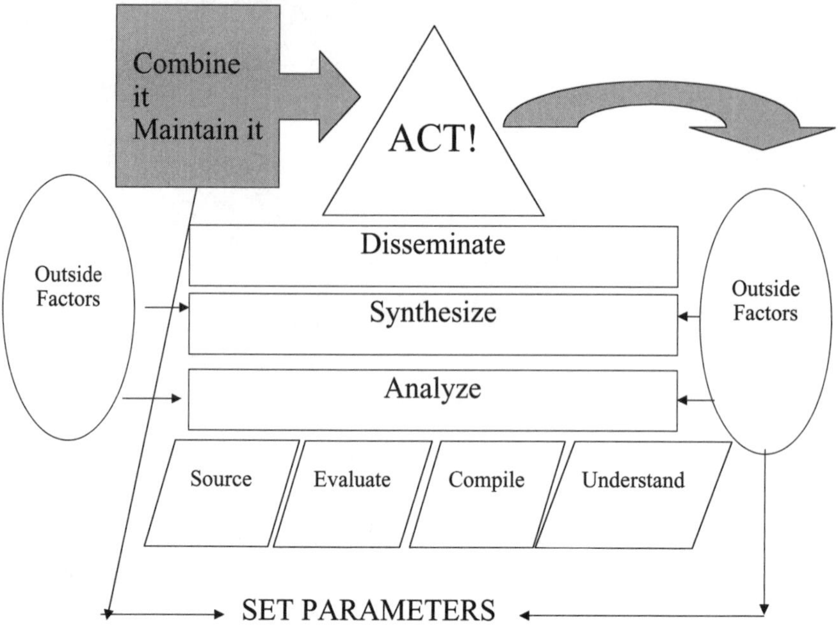

large industry practice at an international accounting firm told his director of research that he had a straightforward request: "Compile a list of industry customers that we lost during the last two years and list the reasons why they were lost."

On the surface, this is a simple request, the answer to which should be found easily in one of the firm's existing databases. On the contrary, in this case the request itself created an odyssey.

The Odyssey

From the very beginning, the quest to fulfill the obligation was derailed by ongoing problems, complications, vague instructions, messy parameters, and confusion. Creating the list itself should have been fairly simple, but the records produced by the firm's systems were in abysmal condition or nonexistent. Neither the practice leader nor his research director trusted the firm's internal reports, so they used the EDGAR database to compare their record with the comprehensive Securities and Exchange Commission (SEC) information.

Auditor Changes

When a publicly traded company switches auditors—that is, when it fires or gets fired by either its current auditing firm—it files a Form 8-K with the SEC stating that the switch is to be made, that the change was instigated either by the auditing firm or the client, and whether there are any outstanding accounting issues with the firm. Approximately 1 in 13 public companies switches auditors each year. These records are accessible from the SEC.

Confused Yet?

Oddly, the external information was also immediately suspect, because it was not developed internally. In other words, this information relied on inputs and parameters that were not under the control of the firm. For example:

- o The EDGAR database tracked only companies that had actually filed a timely Form 8-K. Sometimes, companies did not file Form 8-Ks and sometimes they filed them months later. The firm needed to measure lost clients—all lost clients—on a real-time basis.
- o The EDGAR database reported all lost clients. The firm's partners, understandably, were reluctant or slow to report lost clients to the internal systems, or they did not report them through the correct system, thereby omitting a number of client losses.
- o The EDGAR database measured companies by Standard Industrial Code. The firm measured companies by a proprietary industrial system. The crossover resulted in an omission of about 20 percent of the clients lost, and the

inadvertent inclusion of several hundred clients from other industry practices.

Thus, the firm ended up with two lists, one internal and one external. It decided to reconcile the difference, and asked yet another marketing researcher to do so.

Complicated Enough?

Remember, there were two elements in the original request, one spoken and one unspoken. The requests were basic and brief: find the number of clients and describe why they were lost. Simple enough.

The request illuminates the difference between information and knowledge. The head of the practice asked for the *information*. What he needed was the *knowledge*. His specific data request was, "How many clients are we losing and why?," but that information did not address the issues that the industry head was grappling with. He wanted to know:

- Were there endemic reasons or collective weaknesses that prevented the firm from securing and/or retaining clients?
- Was the competition doing anything substantially different, or had they made any recent changes or upgrades that resulted in a better win/loss record?
- Where did his firm stand in industry wins and losses?
- Was there a "voice" in the collective influencer community that was uncommonly good or uncommonly bad? In other words, had something happened to his firm's reputation?
- Were there quality issues? These are death for accounting firms—witness Andersen's problems in the wake of the Enron debacle.
- Apart from clients, how did the firm do with prospective clients? How did it do in proposal situations? Did it usually win? Why or why not?

In other words, the industry leader needed to solve a host of wide-ranging issues, without delay. His first step in gathering information was to look at the empirical evidence, namely, the lost client list.

Task Goes from Objective to Subjective

We can see that the most objective task—compile a list—depended on many parameters (e.g., cutoff points, such as "When is a loss defined as a loss?") and industry definitions (e.g., "Is the customer in our industry group or not?"). It was subject to the inputs of a variety of people, all following separate sets of instructions. Thus, the clarity of the task receded with each iteration.

Now for the really fun part: Why did the firm lose the clients?

Subjective Slants

The SEC database provided only a limited description of why a particular client left an auditor. In years past, an auditor switch was potentially a signal that there might be problems with the company. Companies were generally fiercely loyal to their auditors. In fact, until the U.S. Supreme Court allowed professional service firms to advertise in 1977, they rarely switched auditors at all. Today, with increasing cost concerns and client perceptions that there is uniform quality among the large national accounting firms, companies create less of a public relations issue if they switch auditors. Regardless, unless there is a substantial disagreement in accounting treatment (also known as "shopping for opinions"), the reason for switching auditors is rarely noted on the Form 8-K.

But the research team had a task before it, which was to find out why the lost clients had switched auditors. The answers lay with one of three groups: the former auditor; the new, current auditor; or the client. There are other third parties that might know the answer (other firms that proposed on the work, individuals who were tangent to the process), but realistically this information could come from any of the first three groups. The research team decided to go to the partners who lost those clients.

It's Never Anyone's Fault

One thing the researchers learned was that the auditors didn't much like being questioned as to why they lost clients. They quickly found that, whatever the reason for the loss, it was rarely the auditor's fault—in fact, less than 10 percent of the time. There was always another reason: risk issues, lower fees, accounting disputes, personal disputes, conflicts of one kind or another . . . the reasons were endless, yet somehow it was usually the client's fault or a situational issue. Nothing is more subjective than a partner's opinion as to why he or she lost a client.

So where did these clients go? If, as the partners claimed, they were problem clients, surely they would not have engaged another Big Five accounting firm. Surely they would have been relegated to the comparative backwaters of auditing, either a second-tier national accounting firm or (worse yet) a regional accounting firm.

The Mystery Deepens

In actuality, 78 percent of public companies leaving the firm chose other Big Five accounting firms, a figure far higher than those firing other Big Five auditors. Only 22 percent of the clients switched to regional firms. The firm was losing clients at a rate twice that of other firms. To all appearances, the firm had major, widespread client service difficulties.

Conflicting Data Emerges

Despite the fact that clients seemed to be streaming away from the firm, contrary evidence existed. On the positive side:

- o The firm's client satisfaction levels were fairly high across the board, ranging from mid-level to best in the industry.

This was true both for the internal client satisfaction surveys and for independent client satisfaction surveys prepared by third parties and industry watchdogs.

- The firm had the highest level of new client signings for entrepreneurial companies.
- The firm signed the most Fortune 1000 companies as clients during that two-year period of all Big Five accounting firms.

However, there were a few troubling data points:

- The firm had lost the highest number of proposals among the Big Five.
- There were signs that the firm's reputation among key influencers had fallen, chiefly as a result of various censures for independence issues and auditing problems.

Of course, information is frequently contradictory, vague, or seemingly without immediate meaning. There were data points that were difficult to interpret or could have had several meanings:

- The firm was near the lead in market share for most industries, but the lead was declining in most industries.
- Although client satisfaction levels were at or near the high among industries, the firm also had the highest level of client *expectations* in the industry.
- The firm had recently acquired the reputation of being the most conservative firm of the Big Five. Although that helped it to avoid Enron-style disasters, and won it kudos from regulating bodies, the reputation hurt it with influencers, particularly those who worked with entrepreneurial companies.
- The firm was third among the Big Five in restatements—situations in which it had to restate the earnings (usually downward) of its clients. This usually resulted in a drop in stock prices. Its average was smack in the middle.

The search for a mere list of lost clients had snowballed into an avalanche of inputs. Data fought with data, opinions conflicted with other opinions . . . where was the firm to go from there?

UNDERSTAND THE SOURCE INFORMATION

The following questions remained for the industry leader:

- If we're so good, why did the clients leave?
- If the lost clients were so bad, why did the closest competitors pick them up?

It is simple to understand information that synchronizes with expectations. But data is often contradictory, particularly when there are myriad inputs. Once the industry leader began to review and analyze the source information, he began to understand it. Answers, data, and opinions can come from a number of sources, but if the reviewer fails to comprehend the underlying meaning of the information, the ultimate knowledge derived will not advance the reviewer's goals.

Seek understanding. Raw data rarely has a single meaning, and it often has many sides. The obvious meaning often conceals a hidden meaning.

Consider the conflicting data that the industry head collected. He received data that was positive, negative, and neutral. He had the opinions of all his partners. He had data created by outside agencies, and he was also bound by his own expectations, desires, and experiences. All these conspired to color his understanding of the information and opinions he derived. Still, after 25-plus years in the business, the industry leader was well qualified to make judgments when collating these inputs.

SYNTHESIZE THE DATA

At the end of a few weeks, the industry head had two separate lists that bore a mild to strong resemblance to each other. He had judgments from about 40 partners as to why the firm lost the clients. He had thoughts from about a dozen different people whose views he valued. He had input from a variety of sources; he had spoken with other industry leaders, with the heads of marketing and sales, and with his regional heads; and he was ready to make the many decisions, large and small, that would integrate the often conflicting inputs into a cohesive whole.

To synthesize the varying opinions, data, information, and news (hard or otherwise), the industry leader started with the hard data. He examined it from all sides, using the opinions of those he valued. He then reached the following important conclusions, buttressed with the hard data:

- The firm had embarked on several initiatives during the prior years. These initiatives had placed a premium on risk management. The firm had become particularly risk-averse to clients in his industry and its win/loss statistics were bearing the brunt of this decision. This was further exemplified by the fact that the highest percentage of clients leaving a Big Five firm and going to another Big Five firm had come from his firm.

- On the positive side, his firm suffered fewer delistings (when a company is dropped by a major stock exchange for failure to achieve minimum exchange requirements) by far than any other audit firm, as a percentage of public companies audited. In fact, its delisting rate was one-third that of its toughest competitor.

- The firm, like the other industry leaders, suffered from resource constraints. It was very difficult to keep strong partners and staff during the roaring economy, when the temptation to defect to clients offered a greater upside.

- During the prior years, the branding of the firm had undergone changes that left the firm with an uncertain market image.

- At least two of the major competitors had decided to invest enormous, unprecedented amounts of money, time, effort, and resources among the clients and influencers in the practice leader's industry. This heated up the overall competitive climate.

○ The firm's market share was strong, to wit:

- It was very strong in the entrepreneurial market. Its share of the privately owned, entrepreneurial company market had increased slightly.

- It still held the lead in the initial public offering market, at the same rate it had maintained during the prior four years.

- It had won the highest percentage of large-scale engagements (companies with more than $250 million in sales). These large companies, however, were only about one-tenth of the total number of public company auditor changes. When it came to the small, risky clients, the firm suffered.

- Measured by assets audited versus companies audited, the firm was still among the leaders in the industry.

○ The industry practice unquestionably faced some challenging issues:

- It had lost four very large clients due to exceedingly odd circumstances in each case.

- As a matter of policy, the firm did not chase small, risky clients for which the fee revenue did not match the potential liability.

- The firm's conservative stance on auditing issues cost it certain clients.

- The firm's four years of record growth had left the partners struggling to keep up with the clients, while other competing firms were schmoozing the influencers.

- The other national firms, as well as regional and local firms, were targeting smaller clients with a vengeance. Industry-wide, there was a significant and accelerating outflow of public company audits to second-tier national accounting firms and regional accounting firms. The Big

Five cachet was no longer considered necessary by many of the very small public companies. Understandably, their market cap was not as impressive as the clients of the Big Five, either.

o The firm was losing proposals, but there were certain mitigating factors.

Clearly, the outcome was mixed, as are most business situations. There were areas of promise and also obstacles to be surmounted.

DISSEMINATE THE KNOWLEDGE

Obviously, no information can exist in a vacuum. The industry head had to disseminate it, or make certain that it was distributed to the appropriate decision makers, senior players, and line-level partners—in short, anyone who would be affected by it.

The industry leader created an internal presentation from this information. It was first given to the firm's overall leadership committee, and then presented to the various industry, group, and regional leaders. Within the next few weeks, most of the industry's partners, managers, salespeople, marketers, researchers, graphics people, and client service specialists became aware of the information, as did everyone who worked at Intergalactic Headquarters, as the corporate offices were known. In short, everyone who needed the knowledge actually received it.

Equitable distribution of important, applicable knowledge remains the major shortcoming of many businesses today. If the practice leader had decided to sit on the knowledge, or to emphasize only the positive or negative aspects, he would have cast a strongly different slant on the information.

ACT ON THE KNOWLEDGE

Ideally, every one of the groups that received this knowledge acted quickly and appropriately to effect the desired changes. In this case, the industry leader commenced with a practice-wide improvement program. His partners embarked on a client expectations and satisfaction program. His marketers began a two-year program to update their skills, targeting efforts, mailings, and events.

UPDATE THE KNOWLEDGE

In the months and years to come, the industry leader ensured that the information was kept alive by:

- ○ *Maintaining and updating the database.* A database has the shelf life of milk. It gets outdated very, very quickly, thanks to changes that happen every day. Address changes, personnel switches, corporate failures, spinoffs, additions, deletions, and many other changes can make information outdated with amazing speed. The industry leader assigned a knowledge manager to run the database and keep it up to date on a real-time basis. On a quarterly basis, an auditor reviewed all changes, additions, and deletions and integrated input from more than 200 sources.
- ○ *Combining inputs.* In future versions of the database, the knowledge manager synthesized all manner of inputs, including client satisfaction ratings, commentary from industry experts, ratings from external clients, and a variety of other items.

In the preceding example, the industry leader faced a number of thorny problems in getting the information he needed to resolve his knowledge shortfall. There were challenges every step of the way, but, happily for him, they were resolved to his satisfaction, and he was savvy enough to maintain the information on an ongoing basis.

WHAT BUSINESSES NEED

Businesses need several things if they are to have successful knowledge management programs. Foremost among them are:

InfoGoals

- ○ Access to information sources
- ○ Access to intelligence sources
- ○ Thought leadership
- ○ Insights
- ○ Accuracy
- ○ Timeliness

Access to Information Sources

Information sources take different shapes and forms, and we investigate them in depth later on in this book. For now, here are a few basic sources that businesses need:

- ○ *The Internet.* Every business has access to basic information sources through the Internet. The ubiquitous Internet is not just an 800-pound gorilla; it is an 8-million-pound gorilla that contains just about anything you need to know . . . if you know where to look. The problem is that any Internet search is like asking for a glass of water and receiving a thunderstorm in response. Or worse, it is like needing a glass of water while in an ocean—it's all there, it's just not precisely what you want or need.
- ○ *Personal sources.* Clients, prospects, friends, influencers, vendors, employees, bosses, partners . . . everyone has an opinion. Some are worth more than others (more on that later).
- ○ *Data sources.* These take many different forms, including various libraries; trade association sources; research firms; data compilers; the print, audio, and video media; media and information capture services (e.g., Lexis/Nexis); and any other source that may be available.

Information is important, but at best it merely provides a base for knowledge. Information, to be useful, must be accurate, timely, easily understood, complete (within its definition), appropriate, and noncontradictory of other sources. Still, having no or scant information undermines the knowledge you are trying to develop.

Access to Intelligence Sources

I once asked one the of the best salespersons I ever worked with to describe for me the difference between a successful sale and an unsuccessful sale, assuming that the salesperson was competent, the product addressed the client's needs/problems, and the decision maker was reached. His answer was illuminating.

"The problem is largely one of equality. The salesman needs to approach the client on his own level. The client is talking here"—he held his hand about eye level—"and the salesman needs to come in at least here," holding his hand at about shoulder level. "The salesman *cannot* come in here" (holding his hand at waist level). "If he does, he's sunk. He has no credibility."

Information gets you part of the way to your goal. Intelligence gets you much closer. Intelligence is useful information that raises you to the level of your clients, prospects, and influencers. It helps you make the right decisions.

Information is important. *Intelligence* is critical.

Management should have the ability to access intelligence sources if at all possible. Who are these people? The short answer is anyone who is smarter than you and knows your business, or has a perceptibly different perspective. This can include a number of individuals listed in the previous subsection on information sources. All these people can offer not just information but also differing degrees of intelligence. Insiders are important; their opinions can add to your knowledge base. They might include any of the following individuals:

- Clients
- Prospects
- Competitors
- Friends

- Influencers
- Vendors
- Employees
- Bosses
- Partners

Thought Leadership

Many managers desire sophisticated, externally produced intelligence on a regular basis. Insiders offer a degree of help, but that is a closed box. External opinions are wonderful sources of additional knowledge and viewpoints. This thought leadership can provide insights from top-level analysts and persons who are expert in their narrow fields. Sources can include individuals such as:

- Top business analysts
- Industry specialists
- Research professionals
- Trade association and industry organization reps

Insights

Philosophically, the goal of a knowledge management program should be to generate insights. Insights keep businesses from stagnating and spawn ideas and viewpoints that might not have been previously considered.

Accuracy and Timeliness

When do you need information, and how accurate does it have to be? Most people would answer the question the same way: They need it immediately and they need it to be perfect. Neither is likely.

Decisions are made on the razor's edge. Degrees of accuracy and timeliness can be offered in commercially available research, but the analysis can occasionally be tantamount to speculation. Also, like any intelligence or information, analysis decreases in value with time. It can also be quite expensive.

RISKS

There are a number of extraordinary and difficult challenges in building information programs. These obstacles can restrain information-gathering success, despite the best efforts.

Limited Inputs

The first risk is a strong tendency to limit inputs. People like to evaluate information and come to a conclusion quickly, and they prefer to deal with a minimum of contributions from comparatively few sources.

One enduring truth is that though one might find a common piece of information or intelligence from several different sources, each source really has a unique take on the subject information. The same piece of information desired (or same parameters given) may generate different answers from different individuals. Sometimes the information isn't compiled in quite the same fashion, or there is some additional commentary, or there is a different perspective.

Be wary of operating with too little information. By limiting inputs, you limit the number of perspectives, the amount of information, and the intelligence that you need to successfully run your business.

Time and Trust

Why do managers actively prefer to operate with too little information? First, they are taught that good managers make rapid decisions, that time concerns are more important than securing all available inputs. Second, they learn not to question ostensibly empirical information; in other words, they don't question the source (or question the source *enough*) as a regular duty.

People have an understandable need to trust their information sources. Therefore, they tend to avoid either questioning those sources too closely or searching for too many alternatives. They tend to persuade themselves that they have sufficient alternatives.

Unlimited Information

Of course you can have too much information, though in my experience the reverse is typically true. Why do some people seem to need every last scrap of information before they can make a decision?

Although it is tempting to procrastinate on difficult decisions (frankly, it's tempting to procrastinate on *any* decision), the customers and the competition wait for no one. When one continues to search for additional information, the issue usually boils down to one of trust: either trust in the information, or trust in one's decision-making abilities. The latter cannot be addressed within the scope of this book, but trust in information typically turns on time concerns.

All risks are, in essence, obstacles that prevent the accessing of timely, accurate information that contributes to your knowledge base. When you match your goals with your risks, you should be able to create all the knowledge you need to fulfill your goals.

THE ULTIMATE GOAL

What kind of information, data, opinions, and intelligence do I need?

Good question. Big question. Tough answer. Answers to this question will be found in Chapters 5 through 8.

CONCLUSION

Achievement of the goals of a knowledge management program depends on your ability and aptitude to gather the appropriate information and intelligence inputs, to maintain the knowledge and keep it fresh, and to use and apply the generated knowledge to make business decisions. Decisions, from the simplest to the most complex, will depend on your desire and ability to complete these steps.

3

Building Knowledge

The shortest distance between two points is a straight line.

It is tempting to use the original algebraic expression at the start of this chapter as your guide to creating applicable knowledge. It is tempting because you begin with a simply defined request or goal, and you believe that it should be quickly and easily fulfilled. But there are three major misconceptions at work:

1. *The question and the answer are easily definable.* Both your goal and the end product are moving targets. Though you may believe that both are fixed, they cannot be treated as such. If you think the answer is in flux, you will usually find that you asked the wrong question.
2. *The information search will resist tangent, multiple, or minor inputs.* Every minor fact, every data point, every casual opinion will cant, refine, or alter the direction of your search. It is rare that a new bit of information will have no effect on your knowledge base.
3. *The pursuit of knowledge is a simple and distinct process.* This is perhaps the most harmful misconception. It is difficult to

constantly question every aspect of the knowledge development process, yet revelation is never easy.

So how do you avoid these misconceptions? How do you find and keep the advantage over your competition? How do you manage your knowledge assets to best drive the success of your business?

CHOOSE YOUR PARAMETERS CAREFULLY

If you don't know where you're going, every road will take you there.

—Mao Tse Tung

This is obvious: If you're searching for information, of course you'll be careful with your choice of parameters. But let's consider for a moment. You can't really know what constitutes your knowledge goal. Therefore, it is difficult to map your search guidelines. What's more, this serial flexibility necessitates that your strategy be very supple. This is particularly important if you have delegated the search.

You are seeking knowledge you do not currently possess. It is only natural to assume that the tactical parameters must be fluid. The key is to focus on your ultimate knowledge goal, in order to drive your knowledge advantage.

THE KNOWLEDGE ADVANTAGE

Your most significant advantage lies in the way you gather, organize, evaluate, disseminate, and act on your accumulated data, opinions, information, and research. Your method will mean the difference between well-founded, solid decisions based on the correct blend of data and opinion and weak choices that will corrode whatever sound business plans you've already developed. In short, it is the difference between success and failure.

THE 10-STEP PROCESS FOR BUILDING USEFUL KNOWLEDGE

There is a 10-step process for transforming information, data, research, and opinions into usable, applicable knowledge:

1. Find it.
2. Get it.
3. Evaluate it.
4. Compile it.
5. Understand it.
6. Analyze it.
7. Synthesize it.
8. Disseminate it.
9. Act on it.
10. Maintain/combine it.

In the body of this section, we'll examine each of these steps closely and show you how to use them to turn data, information, research, and opinions into applicable knowledge.

Your knowledge base is only as strong as the inputs that supply it. Therefore, it is imperative that your search be as comprehensive as possible, and that you use the proper data search tools.

Find It

Building knowledge begins with finding your desired information. Information sources exist at many levels, including:

1. *Internal sources:*
   - ERP systems
   - Internal contacts
   - Peer groups
   - Business owner, senior management, or boss
   - The assistants, secretaries, close friends, and associates of the preceding groups

- Clients
- Formal client surveys
- Employee surveys
- Best-practices databases
- Vendors
- Contractors
- TEC (The Executive Committee) or other associational groups

2. *Basic data:*
   - Mailing lists
   - Research of core data
   - Verifiable financial data (financial statements)
   - Article clipping services
   - Economic data

3. *Intelligence:*
   - Industry reports
   - Analyst pieces
   - Issue analysis

4. *Research:*
   - Industry research
   - Academic research
   - Think-tank products
   - White papers
   - Consultants and consulting pieces
   - Original research and development (R&D)

5. *Technical:*
   - White papers
   - Consulting pieces
   - Trade association information and programs

6. *Opinions:*
   - Expert consultation

- Industry specialists
- Opinion pieces
- Commentary from trusted advisors

Where Can You Find the Best Information? Anyone who has conducted an Internet search knows that there are hundreds, if not thousands, of sources for a specific piece of information. This is one of the most difficult components of creating knowledge: Where should information come from?

Following are examples of external information sources:

○ *Internet pay Web sites.* These are frequently Web sites that have evolved from being free sites into post-dotcom-crash, revenue-generating sites. The most successful firms usually have robust offerings. Examples include Dow Jones Interactive, Powerizer, Hoover's, and OneSource.

○ *Free Internet content sites.* Examples are too numerous to mention, but include search engines, portals, libraries, and other sources of information on the Web. Such sites are generally useful for finding bland, single-category, and stale information.

○ *Major research firms.* These companies concentrate on very high-level industry research and analysis. They create comparatively low-margin research reports and provide high-margin followup consulting to Fortune 2000 companies. The vast majority of their clients are companies in the Fortune 2000 or larger (more than $1 billion in sales). These are large, traditional firms that provide cutting-edge analysis of vertical industry markets. They are the best-of-breed commercial thought leaders. Their research and analysis are created by heavily credentialed, trained analysts who spend their working hours establishing and maintaining their reputations as the brightest thinkers in an industry. They are highest on the informational value chain and are frequently the premier experts in an industry. Examples include Gartner Group, Forrester Research, Meta Group, AMR Research, Yankee Group, and IDT.

o *Data and information firms.* These firms gather easily available data in the form of article clippings, mailing lists, short company profiles, and similar items. Most of their products exhibit little in the way of thought leadership, though they offer useful base data. The deliverables of database and information retrieval services programs are typically limited to basic information geared to fulfilling simple needs or confirming basic suppositions. Examples include Dun & Bradstreet, Hoovers Online, and American Database Information.

o *Investment banks.* Much of their older information is either free or solely for their clients. The information is generally approached from the financial angle, but their industry analysts are well respected. Examples include Morgan Stanley, Goldman Sachs, and Donaldson Lufkin Jenrette.

o *Consulting firms.* Large consulting firms have developed robust intellectual property bases, particularly as to best-practice processes. Examples include Accenture, Bain & Company, and Boston Consulting Group.

o *Think tanks.* These organizations devote considerable high-level thought to issues in nontechnological areas.

o *Research institutes.* These organizations exist purely for R&D and developing new technologies and applications.

o *Independent analysts and researchers.* A number of individuals and organizations contribute to an industry's information base. Examples include trade associations and organizations, freelancers, independent consultants, and others.

o *Top research universities.* The premier research universities are devoted to pure research. There may or may not be commercial applications in their nonproprietary intellectual capital. Examples are Harvard, Yale, Stanford, MIT, Northwestern, and California Institute of Technology.

- *Large corporations.* Occasionally, very large organizations will share information if there is a long-term benefit in doing so.

Perform a Sanity Check. How often does information just look wrong? I spent much of my career working for auditors. In terms of vetting information, even attorneys and engineers don't compare with auditors.

Once you have gathered all the information, perform a sanity check. Many times you will order information, only to find:

- Outdated information
- Inaccurate data
- Fulfilled information requests that are so different from what you originally had in mind (sometimes amazingly so!) that they bear little resemblance to the expected outcome.

And opinions! Everyone has a jaundiced view; each person's own outlook is always colored by experience and expectations. One simply cannot afford to accept most opinions as the rule of law. Try to use at least one other individual to perform a "smell test" to evaluate any new information (particularly opinions).

Opinions are a double-edged sword. Opinions are far less accurate than empirical data, but serve well to refine whatever knowledge you develop.

Get It

Some readers recommended that this section be omitted. After all, how hard is it to get the right information? Well, as with most pieces of the intelligence-gathering process, it's often tougher than you think.

Always question the source. Particularly with a customized search for information, it is critical that information be secured in the original and that the compiler be a trusted source.

If you get the information from a source, or if you delegate the request, you must make sure that it comes to you intact. You do not want the individual who compiled the information to offer you a slanted view, based on either their interpretation of your expectations or their personal feel. Any distortion, no matter how minor, will affect the quality of the information.

Types of contact include:

- *Formal (presentations, surveys).* It's difficult to misinterpret a fully fleshed-out research report. It's tempting, however, for a busy executive to ask others to trim down a report to digestible proportions, or to cite 3 out of 10 sources. Be certain that you see all sides of the issue at hand.

- *Informal (conversations, meetings, Web searches).* Informal data is generally more attractive than formal data because it may be more recent, more accurate, more advanced, and more complex. It is also much shakier and much less likely to survive scrutiny. It is imperative that you question the sources, examining any issue that appears to be outlandish or too good to be true.

Get *all* the information, not just select information.

Evaluate It

Every bit of information must be evaluated for:

- *Quality.* Did it come from a good source, a great source, or an uncertain source? Do you trust the source? I know of two industry surveys, one compiled by a wealthy statistician, one compiled by a not-so-wealthy marketer. For some reason, the marketer's is the more accurate.

- *Quantity.* Stephen King said that a writer should show his work to 10 people. If each one has a different perspective on what isn't working, then the work is probably okay. If all 10 point to the same weakness, then the weakness exists. A viable rule of thumb is that if you hear three different people express an opinion, that opinion is worth examining.

You can usually discount a single individual's perspective unless you really respect that individual.

- ○ *Context.* Perspective is all in knowledge management. How does the information measure up in light of your other compiled information?
- ○ *Age.* Is the information fresh and up to date? Information has a notoriously short shelf life, and it can change any second.

Evaluate any information very carefully. As the old saying goes, "Believe half of what you see and none of what you hear."

Compile It

This goes not just for accuracy, but also for to interpretation. Certainly data, research, opinions, and information have to be transcribed correctly. More importantly, the interpretation must be properly inferred from the presentation.

Information can come in different shades. This is no joke—accuracy is critical. Mistakes and distortions can undermine or even completely invalidate your conclusions.

Understand It

Information doesn't come with directions. It has different meanings to different people.

One adroit office politician had the philosophy that there were enough shades of gray for everything to be interpretable, or understood from multiple perspectives, and that every strong fact had a weak side to it. This was most helpful when he made presentations to typically opinionated audiences. It came to light that his group had lost several high-profile clients during a fairly short period of time. At the same time, the company was in a rather severe analysis-and-evaluation phase of its current client base. He was able to convey the impression that most of the former clients were lost chiefly because of strict and rigorous risk assessment.

Look for the shades of meaning in your knowledge. What does the accumulated knowledge tell you? What does it tell others? What is important? What is not?

Analyze It

To go one step beyond understanding, one has to evaluate information in light of other factors:

- Common knowledge
- Industry standards
- Relationships
- Tendencies to embrace or to avoid change

Does a particular piece of information change your current knowledge base? If so, by how much? Does it completely alter your thinking? If it is powerful enough, perhaps it should—but don't be intellectually promiscuous either.

The key to analysis is to be open-minded. It's very difficult for a closed mind to wrap itself around new concepts, new angles, previously unconsidered information, and fresh tangents.

Evaluation also requires a degree of braininess. This is when most people could benefit from the opinions and slants of a focus group of from one to six very intelligent people. Here is where the genius of a small group can really pull its collective analytical abilities together.

Synthesize It

Information has to be consolidated. A salesperson may have to reduce a hundred pages of information to one page of bullet points. Which are the salient pieces? Synthesis walks the tightrope of precisely how much you should release to a decision maker. This is the key to everything from a basic SWOT analysis to a comprehensive review of your industry.

Disseminate/Distribute It

Information has to get to the right people. This is a huge problem in business, possibly the most problematic of these steps. An entire book could be written about this issue, much of it centered on interpersonal relationships.

As difficult as it is to get the correct information into the right hands, it is infinitely more difficult to transfer information inside a large organization. Information, particularly customized information, may be highly valued inside a company, so it may be:

○ Protected
○ Traded
○ Stifled
○ Hidden
○ Embellished
○ Spun.

All of this lends knowledge capital an internal currency that prevents smooth, frictionless distribution within the organization. This doesn't even include the friction that results from power struggles, feuds, and other clashes in which the quickest way to harm internal competitors is to prevent them from seeing important information.

The executives who can effectively distribute their knowledge among key stakeholders have a huge advantage over those who struggle to get their messages sent.

Act on It

A warehouse of books has been written on the importance of making decisions and volumes have been written on using information, data, and knowledge in decision making. What makes a decision well informed? Why, following the preceding steps, of course!

Maintain/Combine It

Information exists in a vacuum. Data can exist in a vacuum, as can opinions. Knowledge is dynamic, ever changing and free-flowing. It changes two ways: first, the mere passage of time ages your knowledge base and renders it less useful. Your knowledge base must be maintained with the freshest, most recent opinions, information and data. It must reflect currently reality versus old perceptions. Data gets stale quickly. For example, take that most basic bit of data, the mailing list. Within a month, it will be 5 percent to 10 percent outdated. Within six months, there will be something incorrect with 25 percent of the records. After a year, less than half of the records will be completely accurate.

Second, with each new bit of datum, each new opinion, your accumulated knowledge should shift direction. This is especially important in light of a rapidly changing competitive landscape. A single piece of information, however seemingly insignificant, changes a situation *entirely*. One officer takes over from another. A company moves its headquarters or its manufacturing. There is a downturn in the local economy, or unfavorable legislation passes. Any piece of information can change a situation, so it must be reflected in your knowledge management.

INFORMATION BASICS

Map All Trends

I attended a presentation given by the head of sales at a building products company. On one of his first slides, he proudly pointed out that his company had 29 percent market share, leading the pack. He listed his top 5 competitors on the slide, and his next closest competitor was at 19 percent.

His boss frowned and said, "Miguel, I don't have last year's presentation with me. I seem to recall that we were at 33 percent market share then." Miguel admitted that was probably so, and that there were, in fact, a half-dozen new competitors who had entered the market but weren't being mapped. The boss then said, "But Miguel, wasn't the next closest competitor at 15 percent last year?"

Nothing is more frustrating than trying to evaluate a piece of information in a vacuum. If it can be measured against a prior year (or projections), then you have a much firmer basis for analysis.

Integrate Change into Information Flow

A company instituted a client satisfaction process and then struggled along with flat client satisfaction numbers for a few years. The process included three steps:

1. Sign an expectations agreement. Both the client and the company agreed on the scope of services from the outset.
2. Perform the work.
3. Have the client complete a client satisfaction survey.

The company soon realized that it was insufficient merely to agree to expectations and perform a client satisfaction survey. They ultimately decided that the preferable step was to integrate all the information found in the client satisfaction survey into the next year's client service plan.

Every new bit of information, research, or opinion changes the knowledge base of a company.

Measurable Metrics, Trends, and Variances

Information is generally interesting, but it becomes useful only when it is measured, weighed, and checked for trends and variances. Decisions at a glance can be made much more easily when they have some kind of context.

It does little good to generate information and evaluate it as knowledge in a vacuum. Information is static; knowledge is dynamic. Building knowledge is useful only when one can analyze the trends.

Compiling, Updating, and Maintaining Information

As noted earlier, it is important that a trusted source compile the information, data, research, and opinions. It is equally important that this individual continue updating it as well; otherwise, the knowledge flow becomes too choppy and ultimately useless.

Avoid Isolating Pieces of Information

One of the most insidious mistakes when using information is to isolate a particular fact, opinion, or bit of data. There is a tendency to isolate information when a new bit is unique or contrary to prior expectations. Don't get hung up on a single, unique piece of information.

Distance and Information Flow

Distance retards information flow. Information proximity is important. I grew up in Santa Cruz, California, along the West Coast. As can other people who grew up in harbor towns, I could shut my eyes and know about how far away the ocean was just by the smell of the air. The further away the ocean, the lighter the scent. Similarly, the more distant the information, the less the usefulness.

Proximity is critical to information flow in four ways:

1. *Geographic.* Is the information regarding one of your clients or one of your vendors, or is it an overseas trend that may not affect your business?
2. *Timeliness.* Is the information from last year or last month?
3. *Access.* Who can access the information in your organization? If you are the decision maker, but you never see the information, it isn't very useful, is it?
4. *Level.* Who prepared the information? Was it from your closest competitor (high proximity), or was it an off-the-cuff observation by a junior manager (low proximity)?

Making Your Employees Smart

I once gave a two-hour speech on the finer points of business development. What I offered was normally a four-hour course, but I streamlined it for this audience. I asked the audience not to take notes, because we would be covering the information very quickly, and told them that I would hand out prepped notes at the end of my session. Afterward, the boss pulled me aside and asked me not to distribute the information at all. Why? He said that if his employees were to take the handouts, it would be too easy for them to become difficult competitors. In short, he wanted them to be successful . . . but not *too* successful.

Avoid Dead Ends

It is so simple to be trapped in a blind alley. The problem—the pain—in dead ends lies in the fact that no one wants to think that their work is wasted; hence, many people end up pursuing dead ends, dead leads, poor data, and useless opinions. Because it can be difficult to cull information, people end up using these poor inputs.

Information Levers: What Moves?

Robust factors are the major levers of knowledge management. Certain forms of information are so critically important, so robust, that they become the lever that moves your knowledge base. The key to using information levers lies in recognizing them for the groundbreaking, earth-shattering events that they can be. When the manufacturer of buggies saw the first railroad train, did he think it would be the ultimate end of his business?

Avoid Inertia

So many decisions are made from inertia, just because it is far easier to continue a poor decision than it is to make a good decision. The very best outcome of proper knowledge management is that fresh knowledge allows one to act more quickly than one's competitors. Thus, we need to strive constantly to overcome the inertia inherent in our organizations.

Don't Lose Speed

The flip side of inertia is speed. Once you understand the information, act quickly. Procrastination is your enemy. What company, when faced with industry-changing information, will fail to act? Only those companies that will be out of business in the near future.

Risks and Information Flow

Risk management is a popular buzzword, but risk has a significant impact on information flow. Because the very best information flow occurs in real time, it obligates the user to a course of action. Almost always, those actions carry some degree of risk. The successful executive learns to evaluate risks in light of information flow.

When do you play the percentages—and when do you not? It's a trick question. You should always play the percentages, but there are times when fresh knowledge dictates that you act in a fashion counter to the prevailing wisdom. When Joe Kennedy's shoeshine boy started giving Joe stock tips, Joe said that he knew it was time to pull out of the stock market, even though most of his peers remained heavily invested. Therefore, he missed the substantial stock market crash, and all because he was swimming against the tide.

If–Then Decisions

○ *If* my competitor raises prices, *then* I'll lower mine, keep them the same, or raise mine?

○ *If* I find out my best client is unhappy, *then* what steps should I take?

o *If* my customer base is trending away from my product and toward a competitor's, *then* should I sell out to the competition, or should I upgrade my product?

These are all fairly basic decisions . . . but we make many of these decisions each day. How far ahead do we think—how many steps?

Decision Making with Available Information

The very best outcome of a successful knowledge management program is that you can make decisions based upon less information than your competition. You can learn to require fewer data points to have an impact on your markets.

CONCLUSION

The key idea of this chapter is to recognize that all 10 steps in the knowledge management process are critical to the success of your knowledge management program. To review, the steps are:

1. Find it.
2. Get it.
3. Evaluate it.
4. Compile it.
5. Understand it.
6. Analyze it.
7. Synthesize it.
8. Disseminate it.
9. Act on it.
10. Maintain/combine it.

Each of these steps is crucial. No step should be omitted or treated indifferently. It is actually more important to perform the steps correctly than to omit them. If you omit a step, the user of the knowledge will be unaware of the flaw. If the step is pursued half-heartedly, it undermines the value of the knowledge.

4

Intelligence Gathering

The test of a first-rate intelligence is the ability to hold two opposed ideas in mind at the same time and still retain the ability to function.

—F. Scott Fitzgerald

WHY INFORMATION GATHERING IS IMPORTANT TO SALES

The managing partner of a small, local accounting firm once asked me to help him develop his practice. He wanted to speak with area influencers and attorneys and meet a great number of company owners, all in an effort to stimulate his firm's growth. After checking the industry and the firm's reputation, I accepted, keeping the following things in mind:

- Customers rarely change accountants. The nature of the customer/accountant relationship necessitates very close, very personal, and lengthy relationships.
- Most successful people (and this was a successful accountant) have many customer responsibilities and more

administrative duties than they care for; what little time they have left, they spend on trying to get new business.

For three months, our strategic plan confined me to canvassing commercial lending officers for referrals. I had more than 150 meetings with over half of the area's influencers, and I developed 14 prospects directly through the banking contacts. We met with 8 leads and signed 6 customers. My first-year goal was 26 clients and we were falling short.

But where were we failing? The firm's quality was on a par with that of much larger firms, and the pricing was solid. I was getting a few leads, but not a surplus of them. We had a pretty high signing percentage, but I could sense that the vast information machinery behind the prospects, leads, competitors, and influencers wasn't working in our favor.

In fact, we had fallen short in a pretty important way. Most of the assumptions we had made about the market were incorrect. The competitors we thought were solid were fairly mundane, and we missed some very important competitors. The products and services that we had thought would be very exciting weren't necessarily attention-grabbers. The firm itself had a mixed image in the marketplace: not necessarily bad, just uneven from place to place. We also missed many opportunities where a company had switched accountants but had not considered our firm. However, I also saw the foibles of the various competitors.

It was clear that our firm could have the greatest, most cost-effective product in the market; that we could have the best client service imaginable; and that our partners could be head and shoulders above the rest—but if we didn't have information on our clients, prospects, referral sources, markets, competitors, and target industries *and* the ability to analyze, develop, and use that information, our business development efforts would be practically stillborn. Therefore, we plunged into developing the rudiments of an active information-gathering program. This program revolutionized our information-gathering process and the results were astounding. At the end of the first year, we had added 27 business customers as a direct result of our new knowledge management program. Despite an onslaught of competitors in our area, growth of established firms, and what seemed a daily doubling of nontraditional rivals, we maintained a 6-year annual growth rate of more than 30 percent compounded annually. Almost half of our growth was directly related to the information-gathering program.

INFORMATION GATHERING AS A BASIC SKILL

Information gathering is frequently the most mundane, most boring, least understood, and consequently the most ignored aspect of knowledge management. It is also the most important part of acquiring new knowledge. No matter what level of sales skills, customer skills, or people skills you have, without information on influencers and prospective customers you will always be limited by the number of interested parties that you meet face-to-face.

It's no secret that seeking and securing prospective customers is the key to successful growth, but it takes a coordinated knowledge management process to deliver them as actual customers. Information gathering is an activity so foreign to most businesspersons that they usually approach the subject with trepidation, for the simple reason that working with information is different from working with people.

Ironically, when employees move into management, they are expected to become information-gathering dynamos, securing intelligence right and left. But information-gathering training is rarely given in the early years of a career, so the employee infers that communication skills are unnecessary. This results in an apprehensive attitude toward activities with an unclear outcome, particularly information gathering.

Information gathering differs from regular business practices in virtually every aspect. Information gathering is not an activity that easily lends itself to success, because it consists of chasing many tenuous leads before locating any valid contacts. It can require extensive participation in nonoccupational activities, such as meeting people at club and industry gatherings, proving your personal competence in unfamiliar arenas, and promoting the firm's positive professional reputation. It has no clear, definable beginning or end. It is ongoing, and the results are therefore not easily quantifiable, especially in the short run. Because of the vague nature of the initial results, a businessperson cannot point to numbers and immediately declare the efforts successful, or even demonstrate where she is succeeding or failing. A hazy, intangible outcome does not mesh comfortably with the businessperson's orderly world, so she is often apprehensive about information gathering.

The more information sources you contact, the more opportunities you will have and the more customers you will engage. Practice information gathering, and it will become an internalized, natural function of your practice. Of course, you should enhance your sales and closing skills on a regular basis, but an active information-gathering program will create growth opportunities.

EXTERNAL INFORMATION SOURCES

Information can come from either formal external or other opinion sources. One may secure outside information from any of the following sources:

- ○ *External researchers.* External researchers can perform standard research and analysis on a variety of topics. They offer reports and research projects to customers at standard prices. You should have a relationship with at least one external researcher.
- ○ *Librarian service/directed research.* Along those same lines, librarians and directed researchers devote a portion of their time to original research.

o *Analyst access.* Analysts at the premier research and analysis firms charge exorbitantly for their services, so their use is typically restricted to the 2,000 largest global companies. These analysts get almost all their experience in a very narrow industry niche. Currently, these analysts and re-searchers are available only to a few select members of large-scale customers.

o *Name-brand remaindered research and analysis.* One can obtain older, less-expensive catalogued research and analysis per-formed by the large research firms. This is frequently aimed toward smaller or niche markets.

o *Partitioned research and analysis.* Some organizations will sell portions of large, expensive research projects and papers at cost-effective rates. In effect, when a customer requires a chapter instead of the entire report, it can merely purchase the chapter.

o *Anonymous, no-origin research.* A number of organizations market generically available research. This information can come from name-brand research houses and universities, but it may get a "discount" label after a few months or years.

   This is actually quite a common tactic for consumer products; that is, a manufacturer will develop the same product for both its own label and for generic or other labels. Same product, different target markets, different pricing.

o *Independent white papers.* Some independents will create white papers and reports targeted to particular industries. These are separate from independently contracted re-search.

o *Industry trend analysis.* Industry experts often contract to sell regular, independent market, trend, industry, and eco-nomic analyses similar to those available to much larger organizations.

○ *The Executive Committee (TEC).* TEC is a sort of "CEO Corner" where chief executive officers interface with other CEOs (from tangent industries) on a monthly basis. These separate communities are excellent for addressing the information needs of senior management.

OPINIONS

There are three major contact groups that affect each company. Each group receives a different level of concentration and effort according to the desires of the firm's personnel. These groups include:

1. *Actively targeted contacts.* Actively targeted contacts make up a small group of prospects, clients, and influencers that a businessperson personally chooses for development during the course of a year. These are people with whom the businessperson feels a natural link. The number varies, but one usually works on between half-a-dozen and three dozen contacts at any one time.

   Most businesspersons have good intelligence-gathering instincts. They use those instincts best with the few directly targeted individuals with whom they feel most comfortable. Businesspersons have a limited amount of time to spend on developing knowledge. They typically perform best in a setting in which they have established comfort levels with their leads; hence, the bulk of their information-gathering time is spent on these directly targeted people.

2. *Passively targeted contacts.* Passively targeted individuals are those indirect contacts and influencers that are referred to a firm by the firm's network of customers and information sources. In other words, they are friends of friends. They are targeted by management as it becomes clear to information sources, customers, and the market

(through information-gathering activities) exactly what type of information the firm is seeking. The firm's referral network reacts by paying varying degrees of attention (depending upon the amount of motivation provided) to securing information for the firm.

As mentioned earlier, businesspersons use their business development instincts best when they are most familiar with the information sources and have an established relationship with them. Though that is not the case with passively targeted contacts, client referrals usually have such a short decision-making curve that the businessperson is willing to apply her information-gathering talents for the brief period required to get the information—coupled with the guaranteed decision from the potential client at the end of the information-gathering period.

3. *Nontargeted knowledge sources.* Nontargeted knowledge sources offer none of the advantages of either of the previous two contact groups. In fact, they only have one advantage: there are far, far more of them than in either of the other two groups. The vast majority of contacts are nontargeted. No local or regional firm has the resources to contact *every* information source in its industry.

AIM OF THE KNOWLEDGE MANAGEMENT PROGRAM: GETTING AND KEEPING NEW CLIENTS

Exhibit 4.1 graphs the customer's decision to purchase a new product or service over the course of time. When the customer first decides on a new service, it is reasonably happy; then its level of satisfaction can either increase or decrease.

The arc of decision-making curves can vary widely, depending on the business. Purchasing a house can be a lengthy process. Choosing a magazine is nearly instantaneous. The curve depends on the comparative ease, simplicity, and importance of the decision.

Exhibit 4.1   Customer Decision-Making Curve

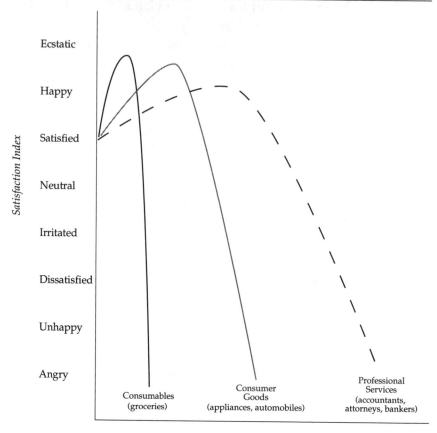

Time

The decisions themselves all have one thing in common: the customer bases its decision on its accumulated knowledge; that is, the information, opinions, data, and experience base that allows it to form a decision. At the same time, the vendor or service provider uses its accumulated knowledge to affect the customer's choices and considerations all along the decision-making curve.

Most businesspersons see the customer's decision in black-and-white terms: Customers are either satisfied and remain customers, or they are dissatisfied and want to switch firms. In other words, they don't see a curve so much as they see two points on the vertical satisfaction index, one at "happy" and one at "unhappy." The most successful businesses realize that the decision to maintain or switch services or businesses is much more complex and fluctuating; therefore, the customer's decision-making curve is much longer and flatter. Typically, the more factors the customer must consider and the more sophisticated the decision, the more time it will take for a customer to become dissatisfied with a current product or service.

This decision-making curve is a double-edged sword. Although it takes much more time for a potential customer to make the decision to switch firms (and allows time for you to cement the loyalty of your own customers), it also means that you can do more work along the decision curve to motivate that potential client to choose your firm. The curve also affects the amount of knowledge you will need to gather about your prospective customers and influencers and the amount of information you will need to convey to those groups. The next section reviews the factors that affect the shape and direction of the customer decision-making curve.

BASIC ELEMENTS OF SUCCESSFUL INFORMATION GATHERING

To run a successful information-gathering program, you need three things:

1. Sources of information, data, and opinions (no shortage there) from your prospective customers and market niches.

2. Information on the businesses competing for these contacts.

3. Methods to actively reach potential customers and influencers.

The key to information-gathering is contact knowledge. Without information on your target contacts, your information-gathering program is over before it has begun. Contact knowledge results from answering six questions:

1. WHAT does a buyer *look* for?
2. WHY does the buyer *seek* a particular product or service?
3. WHEN does the buyer *make* those purchases?
4. HOW does a prospective buyer *choose* among sources?
5. WHERE do you *find* the buyers?
6. WHO should you *speak* with?

WHAT DOES A BUYER LOOK FOR?

A buyer selects a product or service based on its specific needs. How do you identify those needs and how do you address them? An information gatherer may rack his brain to discover something peculiar about the buyer, and he may even stumble over himself as he tries to address that peculiar need. This is a core information need: what does your buyer *want?* This answer changes on a regular basis, and so do its twin corollaries: What is the buyer's perception of your offering? What is its perception of your competitor's offering?

WHY DOES A BUYER SEEK A PARTICULAR PRODUCT OR SERVICE?

What kind of intelligence should you uncover about buyers and their influencers?

Most often, customers change their vendors or suppliers because their expectations are no longer being met by the current supplier. Rarely does a buyer seek alternatives on its own, trying to uncover some small additional service or higher level of service. Ordinarily, a vendor must fail to provide or significantly reduce its appeal before the customer will really consider changing vendors.

Buyers often switch because of a buildup of minor annoyances, things that are too small to be aired: work that is performed sloppily; poor communication; phone calls that are returned late, or not at all; fees billed for ridiculously small tasks. A buildup of minor problems often becomes a major problem, and when a customer has a major problem with its vendor, it will seek to leave. The problem with seeking this kind of prospect is that it is very difficult to uncover these petty annoyances unless one has a coordinated knowledge management program.

Customers also change suppliers because of their own companies' internal changes. Perhaps the manager doesn't care for the vendor, or the new owner of the business wants to use her other friends.

Although there are myriad reasons why a buyer switches vendors, it often comes down to a combination of the current vendor's poor service or difficulties *and* internal changes occurring within the customer's company. In both cases, the knowledge you glean can give you the early lead with the buyer.

The following will shed more light on reasons companies change providers. Be aware of these conditions in your own customers, and be alert to these conditions when information gathering.

Internally Motivated Changes

Internal motivations for change may spring from the company's management, its financial condition, and/or industry business conditions.

Condition of the Company's Management. What does it mean when a company advertises in the newspapers for accounting or book-keeping help? It means that the company has a problem in its internal accounting department. It also means that accepted routine is being altered and that there will be some subsequent change in the accounting department.

Your information-gathering program should have two separate and distinct sides: a passive side and an active side. Passive information gathering covers all the intelligence that comes your way as an indirect result of your information-gathering program, for example, from influencers and ostensibly neutral third parties. The active side of your information gathering encompasses all contacts directly culled from such activities and sources as Internet searches, research reports, and information solicited from clients and others. With either passive or active contacts, you need to know when and why a customer will search for a new vendor or service provider. These factors are called *breakpoints*.

A breakpoint occurs whenever a company undergoes substantial change. The company hiring a new in-house counsel is a breakpoint for a law firm. Hiring a new purchasing manager is a breakpoint for most suppliers. A new C-suite executive is a breakpoint for just about any product or service provider.

What are the particularly lucrative breakpoints at your customers? A company is more likely to seek change when it is already in a state of change. There are several methods for finding this information:

- *Publicly available information.* Management change databases, want ads, executive search firms, management announcements, and other publicly available information often indicate that there are new decision makers at a potential client.
- *Industry grapevines.* Talk to your friends and customers in the industry. Listen to what they say about their competition. Rumors and gossip usually bear a grain of truth, particularly when they concern executive changes.
- *Contact the prospect's employees.* When you talk with a bookkeeper or shipping manager or junior engineer, they will often rail about how busy they are and how nobody has any time to meet with them or help them. Always ask a few probing questions about the company if it is appropriate to

the conversation. Sometimes you might offer some free advice, free help, or free samples.

Remember, this is the information you give out. If the information you reveal implies that you are a problem solver for both influencers and prospects, you're well on your way to a successful relationship.

Financial Condition of the Company. When a customer is profitable, it might search for a better deal. When it is sinking like a stone, it *will* look—a lot. When a company is treading water, however, it will not want to make changes, because every company likes consistency. You can find out about a company's financial condition with four methods:

1. *Keep in close contact with companies.* You should be in regular contact with company employees to discern information like this. Normally, if a business owner mumbles that she "doesn't have time to talk to you" because she is swamped, or because she is out beating the bushes for business, then you should call back in two months. Sixty days is usually enough time for a business to turn around a bad streak or to slow down its shop. If not, try again a few months later. If the difficulties or excesses haven't been straightened out by then, it is likely that the owner either is a procrastinator, or really doesn't want to talk with you. In either case, it is time to remove that person from your contact list.

2. *Keep in close contact with information sources.* They are usually quick to spot when a company is in trouble. Encourage information gathering by your referral network.

3. *Watch the media.* If a company is having noteworthy success or difficulty, you can often find out about it in your local business, finance, or trade media.

4. *Use public information.* The irony about public information is that, even though it is pretty comprehensive, it is usually

very late, and therefore not very useful or applicable in immediate situations. I learned early on that if I waited until a company's problems were made public, at least one competitor would beat me to the punch.

Business Conditions of the Industry. When everyone is fighting and scratching for business, companies will often seek an edge over the competition. When business is humming right along, they do not have the inclination to consider changes. When there is too much business, potential customers rarely have either the time or the inclination to discuss new business with you. The difference between discerning the business conditions of an industry versus the business conditions of a company is that it is much easier to discover whether an industry is taking a beating than an individual company.

Speak with your customers in the industry and take stock of their situation. Try to gauge the performance of a particular industry by calling its association headquarters; speak to the membership director or the person closest to fulfilling those duties.

Externally Motivated Changes

Motivation for change can also come from outside a company. Two common factors include problems within the current vendor and influencer opinions. In some cases, when a company needs to change but doesn't realize it, you may have to provide the motivation.

Current Vendor Problems. During the first year I began gathering information, a full third of our new business resulted from a merger between a large, local firm and the area office of a national firm. The new firm had engaged many customers who were worried (rightly, as it turned out) that a national firm would be too expensive and would treat the smaller customers poorly. In fact, billings to the smaller clients almost doubled, and one August-year-end customer was not contacted by the manager until the end of October—not for planning, not for scheduling, not even to sign an engagement letter! At the end of October, this client received an extension form in the mail, and a cover letter asking that the form be signed and returned.

A golden opportunity arises when the current vendor fails to perform. Even if you have blundered in the same way in a similar situation, this contact is unhappy: all he knows is that he wants a new firm. More than 90 percent of all changes are made because the contact is unhappy with the service to his firm. Service problems can result from mergers, the loss of a manager, a change of ownership from the senior rainmaker to a competent-yet-dull junior employee, or the sudden loss of a valued staff businessperson or a large part of any department. Other, more minor troubles with a firm can be devastating. In any severe situation, there is going to be turmoil—staff leaves and morale plummets.

Obviously, difficulty at your competitors will be a closely guarded secret, but there are a few reliable methods to detect problems at a firm:

○ *Talk to contacts.* If you're open and attentive to your contacts, you'll hear when they have a problem with their vendors. Listen for the hesitation in the voice that signals a problem.

○ *Take heed of industry scuttlebutt.* Industry grapevines have a way of passing on rumors and gossip about difficulties at the competition. If you do not spot problems in other businesses, you need to get closer to the pulse of the industry. Tap it with your managers and staff; undoubtedly, they speak with people at other firms. A smart manager will keep up relationships with other managers just to have a line on high-quality employees. Growing firms need quality employees on a regular basis.

There really is no way to make active contacts for this sort of information without being predatory. Nevertheless, it's a very common tactic.

Incidentally, this route goes both ways. Be very careful about how your company deals with negative news. There is a reason that public relations firms are paid so much money!

Influencer Opinions. On some occasions, an influencer will be so unhappy with the shoddy performance of its client's vendor or the firm's internal accounting department that it will insist on a change. While working with a large commercial bank, I polled the commercial lending officers and found that they referred an average of three customers per year to various vendors for precisely this reason. Obviously, there is only one way to secure customers using this method, and that is to tap into your personal network of influencers.

The Company May Need a Change, But May Not Realize It. Some companies are not motivated to change vendors, but you recognize that they *need* a new vendor. These situations are often the easiest for recognition but the most difficult for implementation. These companies have to be contacted through any means possible.

It is virtually axiomatic that a company with changing needs will complain about the lack of service or communication it receives from a vendor, but will remain with that vendor because the company thinks that it is either too difficult or too time-consuming to find a new one. Once again, a knowledge management program has several purposes: first, to ensure that you are considered when a potential client needs to switch or engage a new vendor; and second, to ensure that the potential client has enough information on you and your organization to engage your services or purchase your product.

WHEN DOES A BUYER MAKE THOSE PURCHASES?

Because of the Earth's rotation and its position relative to the moon and other astral bodies, there exists a period of time when it is feasible to launch a rocket at a particular target. Scientists refer to this period as a *window of opportunity.*

Windows of opportunity exist for vendors as well. There is a period of time, usually lasting from several days to several years, when a company is willing to consider engaging a new service provider or other vendor. A company will usually meet with an alternative vendor that approaches it during the passive window of opportunity. If no one approaches, the company enters a much briefer and more intense period in which it actively seeks vendors. These periods are the windows of opportunity, or breakpoints, when you will most often secure new customers. Your knowledge management program should be geared to identifying potential clients that are entering those phases.

Changing vendors is the kind of decision that takes careful consideration and thoughtful planning, so it is rare that a company owner will change vendors out of the blue. Therefore, breakpoints are often signaled as much as a year (or more) in advance. If a contact shows any interest at all, you should pursue the contact immediately as you are speaking to her, unless the contact asks you specifically to return a call on a certain date. Because a company owner usually considers your firm only during the window of opportunity, it is imperative that you make the most of your contact with her to gather as much information as possible.

If you speak with a contact whose company is past the window of opportunity, you will almost always find that convincing him to consider your firm is impossible. Also, besides the formidable difficulty of this task, after passing the breakpoint the potential client is typically loathe to share information on either your competitors or its decision-making processes.

A company feels most positive about its service vendor when the window of opportunity has just closed. First, when it has just made the difficult decision to change firms, the decision maker is most likely to give the new vendor some leeway. Second, the company has a certain amount of faith invested in the new firm. The businessperson is held in highest regard at the outset of the relationship, and that is when your chances to contact the customer company are the lowest.

Information Dictated by Life Cycle

Windows of opportunity can open at certain times during the life cycle of a company or the company's owner(s). Infrequently, a company will adopt a policy of rotating vendors on a regular basis. You must seek the basic information that will show you when such a window might open, and then cultivate your contacts and leads for followup during the window.

Life Cycle of the Company.   When a company is being formed, or is in its first year of existence, it is not likely to take up much space in your store of information, unless it occupies a unique position with influencers. This is because the company is feeling its way along, trying to establish itself, and is reluctant to change with so much at stake. Time constraints on the owners make deriving knowledge from them a difficult proposition. They are working very closely with their vendors and their relationships at this point are solid.

When the company is from two to five years old, it is growing rapidly and has passed, or is within sight of passing, the survival stage. Your opportunities are the best at this stage, for several reasons. First, if the company is using a sole proprietor, it may look for a firm with more horsepower to take on expanding service needs. Second, its current service firm is more likely to relax its stance on sharing information with others. Third, this is the time that your competition is most likely to increase fees and reduce its level of service, believing that the relationship is so firmly cemented that the owners' loyalty is too great to change. This period of time is perhaps the best time to initiate contact.

A similar situation exists when a company is from five to ten years old, although the company is prone to being set in its ways, and its loyalty to the current vendor makes it difficult to approach. At this stage, it usually takes a drastic change within the company for it to consider new relationships.

When a company is more than 10 years old, changes in business relationships are very rare. Few companies will make switches at this point.

Lifetime of the Company's Owners. Generally, the younger the owner, the better your odds of creating a relationship that generates information, intelligence, and other new relationships. Younger people, quite frankly, are more likely to enter new relationships for three reasons:

1. They are less likely to be emotionally involved with the history of the company.
2. They are rarely emotionally involved with the current vendor and influencers.
3. When they come into positions of power, young people are usually eager to assert authority.

An excellent opportunity exists when the company reins are changing hands from generation to generation.

Get to know the owner's son or daughter or any lower-level decision-maker who will eventually graduate to a position of authority. Many businesspersons take no time to get to know anyone but the C-suite executives or whoever is currently in power. Often, resentment builds on the part of those who are the heirs to the throne, so to speak, and they may form new relationships if for no other reason than to keep the old vendor (which probably still has a relationship with the former decision maker) from interfering with them.

I once attended an economic "state of the union" address where the 34-year-old son of a prominent local business owner was to be in attendance. As luck would have it, I knew him quite well from college, and also knew he was being groomed to take over the lucrative family business when his father retired, probably within the next two years. I walked over to talk to him and we greeted each other warmly. He asked what I was doing now, and I was about ready to plunge in with my carefully worded spiel when an older man joined us. My friend said, "Jim, I'd like to introduce you to our accountant, Tony." I also knew Tony quite well; he was one of the cagiest accountants in our area, and he was obviously covering his bases with the owner's son.

Whenever you call a company and ask to speak to Mr. Jones, and the secretary says, "Which Mr. Jones?" or "The father or the son?" or "Junior or Senior?," you know you are dealing with a firm that will one day pass from generation to generation. Although this is a long-term decision, odds are good that you can sign the firm, and you will have positioned yourself better than any other firm—including the current vendor—by approaching the son as well as the father. The current firm is probably not attempting to generate a new relationship with the son at all, and that puts you in a very strong second place.

Every time I speak to a parent-child team, or speak with a second-generation owner who has taken over the business in the past six months (and I mean really taken it over—not one where the parent is still pulling strings from a distance), I have never failed to sign the customer. When the adult child takes over a business, he or she is likely to flex those newfound muscles and make a few decisions. Because the company's vendor is still tied to the older generation, and because finances are so intimate, the successor would like to have a little room to make some decisions without the hawkish eyes of the parent's vendor around. The parent probably still uses the businessperson for personal work, so the child removes two pairs of eyes from the business by switching firms.

Lifetime of Service. Some companies have formal or informal rotation policies under which they seek alternative service providers on a regular or semiregular basis. Your duty is to find out when these companies are nearing the end of the rotation and begin to develop new relationships.

Change Motivated by Event

Events can also open a window of opportunity. Change motivated by one event, such as a change of ownership, vendors, professionals, or other occurrence, can stimulate change in other areas as well.

Change of Ownership. As in the examples in the preceding section, an excellent opportunity for developing new relationships arises when new owners take over a company. There are possible obstacles, though. The vendor of the new owners may have solidified the relationship by performing a great deal of work leading to the acquisition. Also, both the buyer and the seller of the business are primarily interested in consummating the transaction, not in considering other options.

It is worth your time and trouble to keep up with these arrangements. After the whirlwind of activity involved in setting up a business is over, the principals should settle down and develop new relationships.

Change of Vendors. A customer is most satisfied with its vendor immediately after it has switched providers or suppliers. You will find these companies when, after you give your best pitch, they say, "Darn it! And I just changed last month/two weeks ago/four months ago." Give these contacts a call after the other vendor has had its chance.

One caveat on these customers: Although most customers appreciate a stable relationship, some customers switch vendors on a regular basis. I worked for a firm that guaranteed satisfaction with the work to new customers—but if the customer had changed vendors within the previous three years, it would not be offered a guarantee. If a company has changed within the past year, I require a retainer on all work, unless the company had the previous vendor for at least five years.

Unexpected Events.   What does an unexpected event mean to you? What does it mean to your contact? To his industry? To her influencers? You need to be able to answer these questions.

Change of Other Professionals or Vendors.   When a potential customer changes vendors, suppliers, or service firms, an atmosphere of change exists. This is why referral clubs are so popular. A *referral club* is a group of individuals in tangent industries (one per industry) who meet on an infrequent, perhaps monthly, basis to exchange information of interest to the group.

HOW DOES A PROSPECTIVE BUYER CHOOSE AMONG SOURCES?

At the bottom of the decision curve, when the company is unhappy with its vendor, a contact undergoes a decision-making process using some or all of the following steps. At every step, the vendor is exchanging information, both providing and gathering intelligence.

- ○ *Realization of unhappiness.* The customer reaches the point on its decision-making curve where it fully realizes that it is unhappy with the current relationship. It is not quite ready to search for alternatives; indeed, it would prefer not to sever the ties with its current service supplier.
- ○ *Attempt to repair current relationship.* The customer may try to repair or improve the current relationship, especially if it is longstanding.
- ○ *Search for alternatives.* If the customer decides that the current relationship is irretrievably broken, it will seek

80

other alternatives. This will include canvassing information sources, discussing alternatives with the other officers and employees in the organization, seeking referrals from trade associations, having discussions with friendly businesspersons, and listening to other vendors that have been soliciting the company's business recently.

o *Review of alternatives.* If the customer reaches the stage where it is reviewing the alternatives, it will have between 3 and 15 different vendors attempting to get its business. The customer weighs the strengths and weaknesses of the competing firms at this time.

o *Canvassing of information sources (Part 2).* The customer again speaks to its information sources, seeking third-party opinions on the finalists.

o *Narrowing of alternatives.* After gathering information on the choices, the customer agrees to limit the range of potential service providers to those that fit its specific requirements.

o *Solicitation of proposals.* The customer sends requests for proposal to the businesses that fit its requirements. This is usually anywhere from one to nine firms, and may or may not include the current vendor.

o *Interviews of vendors.* This step, which is usually part of the proposal, is when the customer attempts to establish some sort of comfort level with the vendors who are eager to be engaged.

o *Reference checks.* The customer checks the bona fides of each vendor it is seriously considering.

o *Evaluation of proposals.* The customer evaluates the proposals in light of the references, written proposals, and interviews.

o *Final attempt to repair current relationship.* Quite often, the customer will have "buyer's remorse" and question the need or desire to sever the relationship with the current service firm.

In one case, a company was all set to sign with a firm and just had to take the final step to sever the tie with its current firm. As usual, the new firm composed the letter of termination for the contact. Three days later, the company's former vendor offered a year's free services to keep the customer. Heartbreakingly, but unsurprisingly, the customer chose to remain with the former firm.

○ *Selection of new vendor.* The customer makes its choice after weighing the alternatives.

How to Affect the Decision-Making Process

Would you rather talk to a contact who is extremely dissatisfied with his vendor, or slightly dissatisfied with his vendor? Think carefully. It is actually easier to affect the decision-making process of a slightly dissatisfied contact.

Candor of the Slightly Dissatisfied Lead. The best information you will derive comes from slightly dissatisfied leads. If a customer is just slightly dissatisfied, she doesn't feel an immediate need to consider alternatives, but she is not shy about expressing her dissatisfaction, even in an initial conversation: "Yeah, my guy's okay. He keeps me out of jail. Sure, his bills are high—in fact, they're getting higher. But I've been with him a long time." You receive signals here: The vendor's fees are high. The vendor is aggressive. Their relationship is long-term. Still, there is a subtle expression of dissatisfaction. This contact is indicating that something is wrong, but she usually won't tell you precisely what it is because it would be too difficult to go into it during a short phone call. She would let you know what is wrong if you get in front of her.

Introduce Yourself into The Field of Consideration. It is difficult to overstate how important it is to meet a potential customer or client before your hungry competition does. If you meet a slightly dissatisfied contact, you have preempted other businesspersons from using that contact. By meeting the slightly dissatisfied decision maker, you have enlarged that decision maker's group of alternatives by one—and if you work hard at making yourself a solid choice, you limit the field of consideration. If a contact is extremely dissatisfied, he will immediately solicit bids from five or six different firms. But a contact that is just slightly unhappy will not seek a new firm, primarily because his instinct is to preserve the existing relationship, strained though it may be.

A slightly dissatisfied contact is not immediately seeking a new vendor, so you have the luxury of time to do more work along her decision-making curve. An extremely dissatisfied contact has a wider field of consideration and a much shorter decision-making curve. In other words, she has more options and less time in which to choose. This lessens the impact of the information you are communicating to her, and the intelligence you are gathering from her.

Exert Control over Their Search. First of all, limit the search. If the contact is deeply dissatisfied, he usually initiates the search process and openly courts information from alternative vendors. Generally, a company owner knows little of alternative options . . . until she needs one. She will ask her sources questions like, "Who are the top vendors?" and "Which vendors would you recommend?" These open-ended questions are generally not resolved in your favor, merely because of the numerical odds against any single vendor being mentioned as the best alternative.

Also, if the contact is deeply dissatisfied, he is much more protective of the information he releases. This levels the playing field and prevents you from receiving critical datapoints.

If the company is just slightly dissatisfied, however, you can subtly direct its search process *and* gather much more information at the same time. When this happens, the question a contact asks of the reference source is not, "Who is a good vendor?," but rather, "Is Smith & Company a good vendor?" If the reference source is aware of you (and a good information-dissemination program will ensure this), it will probably give you a good reference.

Second, limit the reference base. A customer that is unhappy enough to actively search for another vendor will seek advice and references from people whose opinion it values and respects. Because of the sheer number of alternatives in any given industry, and the limitations of forming close personal relationships, most people will not refer contacts to you, as they generally favor their own, or the most familiar, vendor.

If the referral source is predisposed to your firm anyway, you will learn about the contact before he begins to look. Why? If the referral source recommends you as number one, he is close enough to the contact to know that the contact should change auditors even before the contact does—he may even instigate it. If, as is ordinarily the case, the reference source is aware of your firm but you are not number one on his list, he will lump you in with the other candidates.

This usually turns out to be the real benefit of sharing information with influencers. An influencer may not give you a contact on the basis of a 20-minute presentation or conversation, but she may give you a good, qualified reference or some critical intelligence. If you do really well in the initial presentation to the influencer, she won't qualify the reference, but will give you a fully positive reference. She is unlikely to refer business away from you, either.

Why? As mentioned previously, no influencers want their contacts to be unhappy with them. It could cost them potential referrals, customers, relationships, and, ultimately, additional information.

Greater Influence than Others

When a relationship becomes extremely strained, the current vendor has usually long been aware of the problems. Your contact's vendor may react badly to a messy break with its customer, and could go to drastic lengths to repair the relationship.

If a contact is just slightly dissatisfied, the current service provider is generally unaware of the dissatisfaction. When the other vendor is unaware that its customer is looking, it has much less time to prepare a countering campaign. It doesn't get to perform relationship repair activities. In other words, the chance is greater that your competition's information-gathering system will fail if your influence is stronger.

Extremely Dissatisfied Customer as an Inappropriate Contact

If a company owner is extremely dissatisfied with his vendor, it may just be that the business owner is difficult to please, is a poor customer, or has little intelligence of value. Although these customers are much more likely to actively seek new vendors, they are also more likely to be domineering, to demand that a vendor do unethical work, and to disdain an established relationship with the current vendor. Obviously, these are the kinds of customers you want to avoid.

In sum, customers who are minimally interested in changing vendors are usually the best customers with whom to build a relationship. Remember, the more difficult it is to build a new relationship, the more likely it is to be a long-term relationship, because both of you have invested so much in it. Psychologically, if the customer has a great deal invested with its vendor, it is virtually impossible for either of you to break the relationship—but these are the customers that will eventually prove to be your most loyal customers.

You are now aware of the motivations, desires, and needs of the modern customer. You should be prepared to recognize these signals in prospective customers—and in your own customers.

WHERE CAN YOU FIND CONTACT INFORMATION?

How important is contact information? I once called on a contact in the computer retailing industry. The contact was very tight-lipped over the phone and wouldn't say a thing. But I arranged a meeting with him immediately, and then called one of our customers in his industry. The customer said rumor had it that the firm had major inventory control problems and needed new accounting software with retail and strong inventory control applications. I located three alternative software packages and presented them at the meeting, with a strong pitch to the effect that we were better for them than their national firm, because we were of the same company size; we hammered at the need for inventory control; finally, I demonstrated the capabilities of the software packages. They signed us on the spot. Without information on the contact, I would not have had a chance of engaging them.

Where do you look for contacts and contact information? You need to use a four-step process:

1. *Develop a list or lists of contacts.* Begin by gathering all the information you can on a particular potential contact or on potential contact lists. Contact information assumes many forms, and can generally be found either internally or externally. A very brief sampling includes:
   - Business Prospector
   - Chamber of Commerce
   - Customer information
   - Direct mail houses
   - Dun & Bradstreet credit and information reports
   - Fortune's business reports
   - Industry information
   - Information bureaus
   - Internet
   - Library information
   - Local trade and civic organizations
   - Mailing list brokers

- Moody's directory
- Manager information sharing
- Professional referral source network information
- Research leads through local business newspapers and magazines
- Staff information
- Standard & Poor's directory
- Social organizations
- Trade shows

2. *Track contact information through an automated database.* No doubt you have a number of automated databases that include general contact, influencer, prospect, and client information. Your database should include the obvious information as starters:

- Company name
- Address
- Phone number
- Company principal (the decision maker, not a book-keeper) and his or her hobbies and interests, along with his or her current feelings about your firm
- Initial calling date
- Initial meeting date
- Followup date(s)
- Current vendor
- Previous vendor and the date of and reason for change
- Their type of business and SIC code
- Their sales volume
- Potential fees or revenue
- Services currently used/products currently purchased
- Track record of calls and meetings with contact
- Decision maker's feelings regarding the current vendor
- Influencers and the contact's feelings about each

3. *Establish personal information for each contact.* Once you have a list of contacts and information on each contact, you need to locate a decision maker at each contact to establish information on them.

4. *Maintain and update your database.* The greatest benefit of any contact database is using it to make the most efficient contacts possible. Without this final step, you don't need a database.

The best knowledge management (KM) expert I ever knew was not the most personable businessman, nor the best technologist, but an individual who had his manual tickler file at his fingertips. Every morning, he checked his list of followup activities, including contacts to make, prospective customers with whom he needed to arrange meetings, letters to write, and references to notify before a prospective customer called.

The worst KM manager I ever knew scorned the use of databases or organized information. Though he was intelligent, he was totally disorganized. If he didn't secure information in an initial attempt, he rarely secured it at all.

WHO SHOULD YOU SPEAK WITH?

In trying to secure information, you are attempting to motivate a company to make a fundamental change in its existing information-sharing relationships. You want it to exchange intelligence with you and your firm. Therefore, you are requiring it to share information. Information is never shared unless you reach the key knowledge personnel.

There are three levels of knowledgeable personnel in every company. Business knowledge can reside at any of these three levels, but there are some identifiable characteristics at each level that will help direct your focus to the most appropriate person.

Primary-Tier Knowledge Holders

If all things are equal, and you know the executives at every level, you will want to direct your initial push to the top tier. This is the primary knowledge tier, and the information is usually held by one of the following individuals:

o President
o Chief executive officer
o Chairman of the board
o Owner
o Managing partner

Certainly, these are the busiest people in the company. They are often the majority shareholders, and can wield a great deal of power, so you can be certain that they will probably be difficult to reach. More often than not, they have less access to internal industry information than someone else in the firm. So why not approach a lower-tier person first?

Many people feel that it is natural to seek out someone on a lower tier—someone with good inside information that will assist you with the primary knowledge holder. Unfortunately, it is easy to get bogged down on the second and third tiers. You can rest assured that these people will probably not contemplate sharing any information of any magnitude.

It is rare that lower-tier people are motivated to seek improvement for the company. They usually do not have the initiative to share information. An upper-tier person is usually more open to a relationship that could help the company.

The background of the primary information holders is often in sales or production; they often founded the company with their own expertise. They may not understand anything about your business, and they may not really want to understand it. If they don't have the knowledge, they will have no qualms about requiring their lower-tier people to seek and share additional information. Lower-tier people are unlikely to drive knowledge sharing, but when backed by the authority of the first-tier person, they will be more open with you.

However, if you approach a lower-tier person first and she doesn't have the authority to share information, she will rarely refer you to the higher tier. She has enough to worry about without considering anything that isn't any of her business. Trying to help you does nothing for her; in fact, it only causes her problems. If she works well with the current contacts and vendors (and she usually does), why should she assist you in establishing a foothold in her company? Even if she doesn't care for the current vendor, she doesn't have the power to bring about any change. Because lower-level knowledge professionals usually screen unwanted contacts, the upper-level authority would most probably be displeased with them for pursuing your firm.

If first-tier people are not seeking to expand their contact reach, don't bother trying to proceed with people on secondary or tertiary tiers; the first-tier person will scuttle your attempts at developing the contact. The only exception is when you have personal knowledge of a clear succession to the company's first tier by a second-tier person. In this case, you should initiate a long-term relationship with the successor to the decision-making position, and contact that person again at the appropriate time.

Second-Tier Information Holders

If you don't know the first-tier information holder, or he refers you to the second tier, you will usually speak to someone with one of the following titles:

- ○ Chief financial officer
- ○ Vice president of finance or director of finance
- ○ Controller

An unsophisticated owner will often refer people to his second-tier arm. This can be difficult if, as often happens, the second tier is unaccustomed to sharing information and/or making decisions. Again, it is much easier emotionally for this person to remain with the status quo.

Generally, however, if a company owner defers this decision to other officers, you should be immediately interested. You don't have to be concerned about using jargon; in fact, the more the better. Professionals often have the annoying tendency to subconsciously talk down to people in industry, so treating prospective clients as equals wins half the battle right away.

Secondly, as mentioned earlier, second-tier knowledge holders rarely get to make business decisions or share business information, and can be timid about changing service firms. The flip side of that coin, though, is that when presented with a rare opportunity to make a substantial decision, some subordinates can actually be more zealous than C-suite executives. They subconsciously enjoy the chance to make such a momentous decision affecting the company—to be close to the action, as it were.

Thirdly, a vice president (VP) does not have as much of an emotional investment as the CEO. In numerous instances, the owner has surreptitiously asked me to speak to a controller or a VP, not because he necessarily wanted them to make the actual decision, but because he wanted to distance himself from the decision. Usually, these owners or CEOs are friendly with outside stakeholders with whom they do not necessarily wish to share information. By routing the decision to a VP, the owner can point to her as the culprit.

Third-Tier Information Holders

The top two tiers represent the company's primary and secondary decision makers, who together hold and drive most of the business knowledge. Needless to say, other decision makers can contribute to your knowledge base, particularly about their companies. Third-tier information holders may include:

- Engineers
- Controllers (if there are identifiable officers at the second tier)
- General managers
- Directors of operations
- Bookkeepers
- Office managers or secretaries

As mentioned, second-tier decision makers are less likely to change relationships than first-tier decision makers. Third-tier people would just as soon turn you down flat. They don't desire change and they don't usually have the power to change relationships. The only time you should contact any of these people is when they are the only route to the decision makers.

Nevertheless, at times you'll need to pass through the lower tiers to reach the higher tier. If lower-tier employees screen vendors, remember that their training is rarely extensive. This means they will react to you almost completely on an emotional level. If they get along with you, if they are friendly to you, you will progress to a higher level. You may be the most competent businessperson in town, but if you rub these people the wrong way, you will have no shot at the engagement. Many businesspersons shoot themselves in the foot by not feeding the egos of these bottom-tier people; consequently, they are shut off from the decision maker.

Initial Contact

When you make an initial contact over the phone, you will probably speak to the secretary first. When trying to get through the secretarial barrier, there are several important things to remember.

First, in spite of the close relationship between the CEO and the secretary, the secretary is rarely aware of the CEO's level of applicable business knowledge. Normally, the secretary has been told to screen all sales calls, and will assume that the boss has an excellent relationship with the present vendor or service provider. Remember, as far as a secretary is concerned, everything is smooth sailing with all established relationships. Secretaries normally enjoy security, so any change, no matter how peripheral, is perceived as threatening and works against you. If a secretary comments about the quality of the current businessperson, don't get discouraged; just try to reach the boss at another time. Secretaries are rarely capable of judging the current relationship.

Low-level personnel will often sing the praise of existing relationships. If a bookkeeper asks you to mail him some literature, do so—and send a copy to the company owner. Make a followup call three days later. It is important that you make the call very early in the day, at lunchtime, or after five o'clock, when the secretary or bookkeeper is unlikely to answer the phone. The qualifications and benefits of both your firm and your knowledge, which may be lost on third-tier people, may interest the principals.

Though people on the lower levels usually have significant business knowledge, people on the first two tiers have the bulk of the information 90 percent of the time. Again, if you know several people at a company, call on the uppermost person. Almost always, these people have the authority, if not the proclivity, to share knowledge.

Keys to Contact Development

As important as it is to recognize the standard characteristics of a potential information source, it is equally important to manage and develop contacts.

To manage a contact along its curve, you must do more than ask if it is ready to change vendors. You must build and develop a relationship to get that company in your corner, and you do this through systematic, regular followup. Try this schedule of followup after the initial meeting, contact, or call:

- ○ Once during the first 24 hours after the meeting.
- ○ Twice during the first week after the meeting.

○ Weekly during the first month after the meeting.

○ Monthly during the first year after the meeting.

○ Quarterly during the three years after the initial meeting.

When pursuing this followup schedule, you *must* do the following six things *every time* you follow through with a prospective contact:

1. Demonstrate your sincere, personal interest in the contact as more than just a customer.
2. Learn something new about the contact.
3. Teach something new to the contact—bring something new to the table.
4. Get the contact to make a decision, even if it is just a decision to decide.
5. Move forward and improve the relationship each time.
6. Make a bridge to the next contact.

CONCLUSION

What makes a contact a quality contact? How can you tell whether you are wasting your time, or getting to know a future customer, influencer, or knowledge source? Concentrate on the circumstances surrounding your information-gathering program. Remember:

1. WHAT does a buyer *look* for?
2. WHY does the buyer *seek* a particular product or service?
3. WHEN does the buyer *make* those purchases?
4. HOW does a prospective buyer *choose* among sources?
5. WHERE do you *find* the buyers?
6. WHO should you *speak* with?

Evaluate each contact within the context of his or her ability to share knowledge and information, and manage those contacts through systematic and continuous followup.

Intelligence Gathering

Things to consider:

- What is your attitude toward information gathering? Is it professional? Do you consider information gathering to be acceptable? Unacceptable? A necessary evil?
- Do you have a information-gathering mentality? Do your managers? Do your employees?
- What market image do you think your firm holds? Is it the same perception as that of your managers? Your staff? The public? How do you want to change perceptions?
- You will need to be proficient in several areas to ensure information-gathering success. How strong is your ability to gather opinions? Do your contacts know the competition? Who are your influencer relationships? How strongly do they back you?
- Is your marketplace data accurate and current?
- Is your rapport with your current and potential customers solid enough to exchange intelligence and information?

5

Competitor Information

And while the law of competition may be sometimes hard for the individual, it is best for the race, because it ensures the survival of the fittest in every department.

—Andrew Carnegie

YOUR COMPETITION: COLLEAGUES OR ENEMIES?

You are in a competitive business that will only become more competitive, and information on your competition is crucial. Although you should think of other businesses as your colleagues and treat them as such, you must realize that they are indeed your strongest competition. If it offends your sensibilities to treat fellow businesspersons as competitors, ask yourself this question: Would a competitor hesitate to engage one of your customers?

Most businesspersons realize that virtually every part of their practice is contingent on the corresponding aspect of the competition. Your service mix, fee level, customer base specialties, dress, firm image, location, and staff—everything is influenced by your competition, whether you aim to set yourself apart from them or to more closely identify with them.

Competitor knowledge bears strongly on your business decisions. Do you attack your competition in a given market, or do you ignore it? Should you secure a price advantage over your competitors? Should you employ misinformation? Who are your closest competitors, and, more important, what do they have that works? Where are they moving? What are their current services, and what new services are they developing that will appeal to your customers or potential customers? How will this affect your customer mix and your service mix?

One makes surprisingly few decisions without considering the effects on and reactions from competitors. The effectiveness of any decision you make is supported by the competitor knowledge you take into account. You need to dispassionately assess your firm and understand how deeply your competitors have penetrated your markets.

Competitor knowledge in any business constitutes a sizable advantage. I have examined many successful and unsuccessful businesses in depth, and though each had its own strengths and weaknesses, I can unequivocally state that every one of the successful firms had substantial competitor knowledge; every one of the less successful firms either did not study its competition, or it ignored its knowledge. Because information is often a closely guarded secret in our business, competitor information is of tremendous value.

GATHERING INFORMATION ON YOUR COMPETITORS

When Procter & Gamble sees that its competitors are gaining shelf space, or consumer surveys list market share on a pie chart, they are tracking exactly how their own products stand in relation to the competition. They can walk into a grocery store and know their competitors' prices; in fact, because of high initial information-gathering outlays, large companies usually know a great deal about competitors' new products before they hit the shelves.

Through consumer surveys, a company can discern the tastes of fickle consumers as soon as they change. Companies spend millions of dollars on consultants who map trends, and millions more on firms or in-house departments that gather competitor knowledge.

Of course, though superficial competitor intelligence is simple to obtain, the very nature of business dictates that extensive competitor intelligence is next to impossible to secure. Businesspersons are secretive about most information, including pricing levels, customer base, their products and services in development, and even the names of their employees.

Information on your competition is of much higher value in a service industry than in a product business. Every speck of information you have on your competition gives you an advantage, because service delivery is of the greatest value to the consumer.

The interesting thing about service industries is that one's reputation is key to a potential customer's decision. Outside opinions of your work are often the determining factor when a prospective customer considers your firm. With a product, a contact can compare the strengths and weaknesses of tangible items. In contrast, a company owner is rarely able to draw on technical knowledge when deciding between auditors. The perception of a business by the potential customer base *is* that business's reality.

SOURCES OF COMPETITOR INFORMATION

It is not too difficult to gather general information on your competitors. To discover generalities, all you need do is check public sources, such as industry publications in the market area; or ask professional and trade organizations to identify firms that specialize in that industry. For instance, if you specialize in contractors, check the various local contractor trade associations to see which businesses are members. Then ask those members which accounting firms they use. This method will reveal exactly who the competitors are in your market segment.

Gathering specific information is more difficult, though there are effective methods. You need reliable sources of information on your competitors. These sources include the following.

Potential Customers

Meeting with potential customers is a perfect opportunity to uncover pertinent information concerning your competition. The nature of the customer/manager relationship dictates regular, timely client interaction by your competition. A potential customer has reason to reveal why it is changing service firms, what it likes, what it dislikes, the nature of its relationship with the vendor, and other revealing information. Potential customers may also ramble on at length about things that would otherwise never come to the attention of people in the industry. They may comment on both their current vendors and the firms currently competing for the work.

Any information you gather during your interaction with customers will benefit you in the future. You must realize also that your relationship with your customers is a two-way street. The access that you give them to the inner workings of your firm may be revealed to others.

Manager/Current Staff Interaction

At an absolute minimum, firm principals and staff should attempt to discover as much about their competition as possible, even if this merely entails trading anecdotes. People in any business actually know a great deal more about their market than they realize, and a pooled body of knowledge from both managers and staff could be formidable indeed. If you don't already have one, begin written profiles of all your geographic competitors—not just the major concerns, but *every* competitor in your area of concern.

New Staff

Every employee who comes from another firm should be debriefed. When they arrive at your firm, they should go through an intensive information-gathering session with their supervisor regarding their views of the marketplace. This is not to say that the new employee should provide names of customers who are dissatisfied with the employee's former employer. The point is that an informational meeting with their supervisor is a productive means for gathering information and should not be neglected. Generally, firms hire people from other firms similar to their own, so such a meeting is a natural and ideal method of gathering information. By the way, this is another reason for your employees to remain close to the employees they knew from other firms, industry functions, and college; the accounting industry is a provincial community, and people do relocate.

New Customers

When you are hired by a new customer, ask to see the proposals of the firms that competed for the work. A proposal is one of the most revealing documents a business can prepare about itself, as they are essentially 4 to 10-page resumes addressed to a prospective customer. Most businesses assume that a contact wants to know as much as possible about their practices, and thus the firms try to provide "snapshot" images, listing such sensitive information as: manager and staff resumes; pricing structure; the history of the firm and its managers; the predicted completion time of the engagement; expected fees; guarantees offered (if any); a breakdown of estimated chargeable hours; industries in which the firm specializes; specific areas of expertise; and other such items.

Proposals not only provide information about competitors, but you will also discover comments by the predecessor accounting firm and the customer on the strengths and weaknesses of the predecessor firm. Your general and specific knowledge about several competing businesses is thus broadened with little effort. New customers and new employees are your two most up-to-date sources of information on competitors. To the extent you feel comfortable, interview those with whom you have just formed new relationships. Remember that your new employees have developed business relationships too.

Local Information Sources

During my first two months in a large regional accounting firm, I did a study of the local commercial bankers and our competitors. Before speaking with the bankers, I asked the managers of my firm to identify our toughest competitors. After lengthy discussion, we named several firms. Then I canvassed the area's commercial bankers, and found some interesting things during the conversations. The managers and I felt that three competitors in particular had the highest quality of service and technical proficiency in the area—but none of the bankers even mentioned their names. When I asked the bankers who they perceived to be the best accounting firms in the area, I was in for another surprise.

More than 75 percent of the bankers named the two local firms with the highest fees (their fee schedules were 40 percent higher than the median). Neither of the firms noted by bankers was included in the original list of competitors that the managers and I had developed. So you can see that your perception of your competition and the perception of the market makers and information sources may differ markedly. You need to be aware of how the market feels about you, and how it feels about your competition.

This is also a great way to gather information on your competitors. Don't ask which firms the bankers refer business to, or who your toughest competitors are. This will only put them on the defensive, and is certain to keep them from answering your questions. Merely ask who they consider to be the best in the business.

Information-Gathering Research

Some firms have taken to sponsoring information-gathering surveys and sharing the results with participating firms. They usually have low returns and the information is of dubious value. Such surveys are generally anonymous, though that rarely appeals to businesses. It seems that most businesses would rather be unaware of their markets than benefit from market research.

Two research avenues are open to you. First, note the research that comes from your state associations and societies. Secondly, employ an information-gathering intern from a local university for customer and competitor survey research.

Information-Gathering Program Input

One attractive side benefit of an established information-gathering program is the ability to gather, record, and utilize knowledge about your competition. One firm developed reports on the state of its competition on a regular basis, categorizing its closest competitors in five ways:

1. *Aggressive information-gathering firms.* These were firms making a significant push in the report sponsor's market area. Signals included:
   - Advertising
   - High number of proposals on competing engagements
   - High number of customers recently switched to that firm
   - Other firms purchased by or merged with that firm
   - Recent personnel ads in the classified section
   - Sponsored seminars
   - Speeches
   - Written articles
   - In-house newsletters

- Membership in organizations with aggressive lobbying for top positions
- Increased referral source contacts
- Teleinformation gathering
- Direct mail programs
- Increased exposure at local business functions.

The total number of firms on this list was usually limited to between 2 and 5 firms out of more than 450 competing firms in the market area.

The reason so few firms appear on such a list is that it is difficult to maintain a serious, aggressive information-gathering posture on a sustained basis. It is draining on the resources of the firm, though it is usually more draining emotionally than physically or financially. One might say that information gathering is an acquired taste.

2. *Notable information-gathering firms.* These firms employed the same or similar methods as the firms on the top list, differing only in the degree to which they utilized the methods. For instance, instead of an in-house newsletter, a firm on this list might use an externally prepared newsletter; or, instead of seven or eight of the information-gathering signals, they would exhibit three to five signals. There were usually between 8 and 12 firms on this list out of about 450 firms.

3. *Passive information-gathering firms.* These firms also used the same information-gathering tools; however, they limited themselves exclusively to passive tools, which means they excluded newsletters, direct mail, and teleinformation gathering. They did not actively reach out to the market. Their exposure at functions was more limited, and they performed no activities that required a good deal of time, such as producing an internal newsletter, writing articles, or making speeches. They restricted their efforts to public

relations, limited mailings, quotes in accounting and tax articles, and work with local charitable, civic, and community organizations. These firms practiced the traditional approach of businesses that wish to grow, but invest a very limited amount of time in doing so.

This style of information gathering is not nearly as successful as active information gathering, but it is an acceptable alternative for firms with reticent management or managers whose time is primarily consumed with administration and customer relations. Essentially, firms that lack the time or inclination to pursue aggressive information-gathering programs will prefer to adopt a passive information-gathering stance. In the study area, this group consisted of about 30 percent of all firms.

4. *Content firms.* As the title implies, these firms rarely seemed to sign new customers, though they rarely lost existing customers. Aside from excellent customer relations, they did virtually nothing to attract new business. Every customer included in the survey seemed to have been with the firms for 10 years or more.

   In terms of competition, these were the firms about which we usually worried the least. As a rule, they were old-line firms run by traditional practitioners who rarely undertook any information-gathering activity and were fiercely protective of their customer bases. Their fee levels were usually 10 to 30 percent below the market average, and they exhibited no interest in increasing the size of their customer base. They were the least likely of the 5 categories to be a threat to anyone, and constituted about 65 percent of the studied market.

5. *Shrinking firms.* Shrinking firms are probably the most dangerous in terms of pure competition. These firms tend to be directed by managers who are either very young, incompetent, overburdened, or heading out the door.

If a company is seeking to close, it usually prepares for an orderly disposition of its customer base through sale or referral, and its departure from the market rarely causes a stir. However, firms headed by incompetent or overburdened managers are more likely to develop overly aggressive, extensive information-gathering programs; use tactics of questionable ethics; or use such radical tools as consistent misinformation to shore up their failing practices. There were usually half a dozen to a dozen of these firms on the study list at any one time, and their unpredictability was enough to cause concern. Like cornered animals, these firms were most dangerous when trapped. Some of their dubious methods included the following:

- One business hired a local MBA student for information-gathering research. Her temporary position was an internship arranged through her university. The project was aimed at securing sensitive information from the other businesses in the market. The intern assembled a 15-page survey of the most sensitive questions possible and addressed it to the 100 largest businesses in the area. On the front page of the survey, she identified herself as an MBA student who would be using the information for a research project for her information-gathering class. She did *not* disclose that the information would be available to the managers at her business, nor did she mention that she worked for the firm; in fact, there was no mention of the firm anywhere in the survey! She also mentioned to me that, although the survey was supposed to be anonymous, only 2 of the 70 respondents failed to return the survey in a firm envelope, the origination of which she dutifully noted for her managers.

- A business performed Dun & Bradstreet checks on all its contacts, and also on its most significant competitors. The firm even convinced its most trusted customer to solicit proposals from its 10 most significant competitors in the area; in return, it performed the annual review at half price.

- A business placed bogus classified advertisements in local accounting journals to see who was searching for help, or for merger or purchase candidates. Some firms also search the Sunday classifieds for firms that are recruiting accounting help, whereupon they target those firms' customers.

- A business helped a local business periodical compile a "Top 100 Private Companies" list. Although the list was to use gross sales as a barometer, the questionnaire encouraged "all companies that had more than $1,000,000 in sales" to respond (the smallest company on the list did more than $15,000,000 in sales). Further, the questionnaire requested not only the level of gross sales, but also the name of the principal, the current business, and the company's fiscal year end!

There are many ways to collect market information. Needless to say, it reflects negatively on you and your profession to employ unethical methods—not to mention the potential for losing one's certification or suffering other disciplinary actions.

WHAT YOU SHOULD KNOW ABOUT
YOUR COMPETITION

You know *why* you should know about your competition, but *what* should you know about competitors? Obviously, the more you discover about a competitor, the greater your edge in competing for customers and planning your services. For most of your significant competitors, you will want to know all you can. The remainder of this chapter describes the most useful areas of information.

Names of Competing Businesses

Many businesses only know a few of their closest competitors. It is important that you be aware of all businesses in the market, including the firms that are on their way up and those on the way down. In one business that had an exceptionally aware information-gathering sense, four of the five managers were knowledgeable about two dozen of their top competitors.

Headquarters and Offices

Customers often consider the location of their service providers to be important. Know which firms have physical headquarters in your immediate geographic area. Emphasize your proximity to a customer during negotiations when you have that advantage.

Every so often you may run across the name of a business in your market area that you do not recognize. Usually its headquarters are just outside your normal market area, and its market base overlaps your area. If this firm submits a proposal to a prospective customer when you do, you will be at a disadvantage if you're unaware of that competitor's strengths, including its physical proximity.

Performance Trends

Many firms gauge the quality of their competitors by one-shot information, or by information that is more than a year old. A historical snapshot of an business is not worth much. Concentrate instead on charting the progress of your competitors over the years. Who is growing? Who is shrinking? Who has lost key people? Check the business section. Who is setting up new services? Who is retiring? It is easy and valuable to maintain a simple, updated progress chart. The four best sources for locating trend information are: (1) your professional referral network; (2) your friends and acquaintances in the industry; (3) new staff hired from other firms and new customers secured from other businesses; and (4) press releases and local business journals that include trend information.

Financial Condition of Other Businesses

This type of information is usually secured only through rumor. The only benefit in it is the knowledge that a firm in financial trouble is in a poor position to grow. You can almost always remove this particular firm from your list of tough competitors.

The sole exception to this rule are companies that combat financial problems by embarking on a crash crusade to secure new customers. Though this is one of the greatest mistakes a company can make (it brings in no additional revenue, but requires time and money at the outset that will hasten the firm's decline, it is a serious threat and your firm can get hurt. Crash sales efforts can willfully or inadvertently harm established firms, even though disaster will eventually occur for the declining firm.

Price Structure and Responses to Price Competition

This information is usually garnered from new customers, new employees, and your referral network. Remember, different firms have different responses to price competition. Some firms take the purely professional approach and do not lower their fees when a customer gives a competitive price/fee proposal. Other firms will slash or match competitive rates in an effort to retain the customer. Occasionally, when their fees decrease, their service also decreases and the customer is still unhappy. Learn the various responses of your competitors.

When evaluating the pricing structure of a competitor try to identify your competitors' costs. How low will they reduce price? How likely are they to write up or write down an engagement? Will they lowball fees to keep a customer? Get a handle on their procedures.

Key Members of the Company

Of course, the CEO immediately comes to mind when you investigate a firm's key people. But when C-suite executives near retirement age, they are actually among the less important players. What you need to consider is: Who can't this firm do without? Who are its most valued employees? Which employees will be considered for promotion? These are the influential people you need to maintain contact with through the years. These businesspersons may become managers and keep their firms growing; or they may not make manager, get frustrated, and open their own shops in competition with your firm. They could even end up working for you one day!

What are the idiosyncrasies of top management? Do they have legal problems? Money problems? One of the largest independent businesses in the study area lost 25 percent of its practice because the managing manager was billing too high and spending too much money. The firm's own infrastructure threatened to crush it, so it merged with a national firm.

Which managers give poor service? There is a wide range of manager types in a business and their quality can differ drastically.

One final note: Be aware of the firm's reputation as an employer. Troubled firms that have high employee turnover tend to have high customer turnover as well.

Competitor Target Markets

Knowing a competitor's specialties and target markets can be useful in the long run. If a close competitor arranges a specialty in servicing subcontractors, it is a good bet that it will support the new program with a strong information-gathering program designed to maximize the firm's exposure to subcontractors. When a firm organizes a new specialty, it is best initially to concentrate on other markets. Keep close to the pulse of the marketplace and see how well the erstwhile competitor performs. If the firm succeeds, it will consolidate its grip on the marketplace; but if it fails—or, more accurately, if it cannot deliver everything it promised—there will be fallout. This is the flip side of new services and specialties. If they don't "take," you are in danger of losing the customers you signed as a result of those new services and specialties, to say nothing of the subsequent damage to your professional reputation.

The second largest independent business in our area had experienced slow growth for several years and was anxious to stimulate more vigorous growth. Our area was flush with law firms and new companies, and as legal battles began to intensify, that large business identified litigation support as its next big area of growth. Unfortunately, so did at least six other local firms, not to mention the national firms with existing litigation support departments.

The firm hired three expensive, heavyweight, litigation support specialists to develop the department, two of whom were made managers immediately. Then things began to fall apart. With so many firms joining the fray, fees declined as firms jockeyed for position. Competition among the national firms heated up, and they expanded their own litigation support departments. The large firm that had identified what it thought was open territory found itself in the midst of a feeding frenzy. It overcompensated and threw more resources into litigation support even as service for its existing customer base declined. In one year, it lost 25 percent of its customer base.

Unique Features of Competitors

Bells and whistles don't usually sway customers too easily. However, it is important to note that when you are submitting competing proposals, you should emphasize your unique features over those of other firms. Trumpet the seemingly small differences that other accounting firms do not have, do not consider having, or do not even think worth mentioning. It is, of course, crucial to be able to match the features of your competitors when information gathering for the same customer.

Short- and Long-Term Strategies

Unless you get a peek at the competitors' information-gathering plans, it is almost impossible to uncover their strategies without long-term examination of their market moves. In general, the best you can do is to extrapolate competitor strategies from their market actions and market rumors. By knowing their future moves, you can tailor your own strategy to effectively counteract your competitors' strategies.

Sustain or Grow?

The majority of businesses either are simply not in the growth mode, or are in passive growth modes, which means they take on new customers only when approached. Firms that are content to maintain their market position rarely react strongly when they lose the occasional customer.

You need to be aware of the companies with aggressive information-gathering plans. These companies will vie for position with your professional referral network and will use active information-gathering techniques. It is essential that you match the customer service trappings these companies offer, or you will find yourself in the unenviable position of competing for customers (possibly your own!) with fewer strategic options.

Competitors That Target Acquisitions

Businesses that aggressively market their services and target other firms for acquisition will prove to be your most difficult competition by far. Passive firms rarely contemplate either purchases or mergers.

Some competitors will make acquisitions, but will either be unable to handle an influx of customers, or will have made the acquisition for the wrong reasons. You do not need to worry about these firms. In fact, you should position yourself to take advantage of a failed merger's fallout.

At the first sign of a purchase or merger in your geographic market or specialty area, it is time to get concerned—not when your competitor's new facility or addition is already up and running. Huddle with your managers and discuss how best to meet this new challenge.

Companies with a goal are dangerous competitors. In 1983, the local office of the weakest national firm merged with the most aggressive independent local firm and the result was an office that set the local market on its ear. The new office transformed from a no-growth, content firm into an aggressive, information-gathering-oriented firm. The first year, which is normally a year of acclimation, saw the new firm lose 15 percent of its small business customers—but realize a net $1 million fee gain for the year.

Another example is an aggressive firm, with a heavy concentration in manufacturing, that purchased a passive firm specializing in construction. Soon afterward, every contractor in the area that was not already a customer was being contacted, and the firm achieved huge growth.

Keep these examples in mind, even if you are not considering an acquisition. You should be aware of potential mergers, purchases, or newly established businesses, if only to protect your own customer base.

New Competitor Products and Services

Each new product and service dramatically increases an business's potential market base. More important, the more products and services you have, the more appealing your firm is to rapidly growing customers, which is the type of customer every businessperson wants to have.

Every time an aggressive competitor adds a service, she needs to justify that service with new customers. New customers don't grow on trees, so she must solicit or contact them as quickly and effectively as possible. Obviously, no businessperson with a new service will keep it a secret. You can depend on a crowded marketplace every time this occurs.

Delivery Time

When does a customer want his product? Preferably the day after he gave you the order. Turnaround time is a crucial determining factor for customers. When making a proposal or speaking with a contact, knowledge of its current firm's turnaround time can either qualify the company as a contact or remove it from your list.

Level of Quality

Quality is difficult to discern, because there are different skill levels between competitors. It is virtually impossible to do so industry-wide. What is important is the ability to gauge your own level of quality. If the subject work is a particular specialty of yours, the contact must be made aware of that fact in no uncertain terms.

Strengths and Weaknesses

Knowing the various strengths and weaknesses of your competitors gives you two complementary advantages. First, it frees you from wasting time and resources attempting to enter markets that, realistically, are closed to you because of a competitor's strengths. Second, it allows you to focus your information gathering on markets that hold greater promise.

Resolution of Customer Problems

Can your competitor resolve customer problems quickly and efficiently, with no loss of customer respect? This is one of the most critical yet most ignored problems afflicting businesses. No one likes to admit that her firm falls short in any area, least of all customer service, and this myopic view is responsible for the majority of customer defections. Many people have a nasty tendency either to consider customer complaints to be the customer's fault; or worse, no matter what the complaint, to assign it no priority.

Learn from your new customers. Find out what they liked and did not like about their former firms. In this way, you will have a road map for preferred treatment of these customers, and you will get to know their former vendors' strengths and weaknesses. You can position yourself to exploit these weaknesses with future contacts.

Have You Ever Taken Business from Them?

Which of your customers used the competitor in the past? How did you beat the competitor? How will you beat it in the future? This is what you do with the results of your competitor knowledge program. Every competitor file must include an entry on the competitor's weaknesses, the competitor's strengths, and how they were overcome.

What Accounts Are Their Best Relationships?

I once secured a customer that a national business had discussed openly in a publication. Now, one would assume that if a customer is discussed in an article, the customer-manager relationship is close. If this is true, though, one might wonder how well the firm services the rest of its customer base if a close customer leaves.

Normally, you should avoid gathering information from a competing firm's best relationships. These contacts may tell their vendors that you are information gathering from them, and may string you along or use you to improve their situation with their own vendors.

What customers do other firms have that you want? Some firms have a customer mix that is incompatible with your customer structure. Most firms have some customers that you cannot service. Keep track of which customers use which firm, and figure out whether you can service them.

Which Customers Are Likely to Leave?

This is the entire point of an information-gathering system. Your competitor knowledge and information-gathering programs will be geared to finding these opportunities.

What Is the Firm's Reputation in the Business Community?

It is difficult to take business away from businesses that have high standing in the business community. If you contact too many customers from these firms, you may find your professional network referring business elsewhere. This is a twist on the old adage that the "enemy of my friend is my enemy."

How Does the Customer (and Community) Perceive You?

A positive public image is critical to your firm's growth and success. But when your firm is rapidly rising, other businesses will target your customers as contacts: they will target you in the contact marketplace competing for customers; they will undermine you among professionals when competing for referrals; and they may even lowball your customers so as to have a reference point for other contacts.

KEEP A CENTRAL DATABASE

When you have gathered sufficient information on your competition, keep it in a central data file. Automate the file if at all possible, and keep it open to your managers and employees. This will enable them and you to have a profile of a potential competitor immediately available.

CONCLUSION

Everything you should know about your competitor amounts to everything you would *not* want a competitor to know about you.

Competitor Information

The importance of updated and accurate information on competitors is absolute: The less access you have to competitor information, the more you restrict your options, and the less certain you are of your decisions or the direction in which your firm is proceeding.

Obtaining competitor information may seem difficult, or may appear to require too much time and energy. As with any new plan, time is required, but the process becomes easier and more effective as you become accustomed to it.

A good approach to gathering competitor information is to investigate and choose activities from this chapter. As these processes become easier for you and a natural part of your information process, you can upgrade and add your information to an easy-to-use database.

6

Customer Relations

A doctor can bury his mistakes, but an architect can only advise his clients to plant vines.

—Frank Lloyd Wright

For obvious reasons, your customers should be your best sources of intelligence and information. They are key contributors to your knowledge management program. They are your customers because—somehow, some way—you have managed to fulfill their needs and expectations.

Your first goal is to keep your current customers happy, ultimately bordering on ecstatic. The happier your customers, the more likely they will be to share information and business intelligence with you.

WHAT CONSTITUTES GOOD SERVICE?

The more important question is "Why is good service critical for an open information flow?" Good service is predicated on one thing: excellent communication. It is the foundation, the cornerstone of ensuring client satisfaction; equally important, it fosters the critical climate of trust necessary to generate open information.

So what, exactly, do customers want?

WHAT DO CUSTOMERS WANT?

Every businessperson who ever lost a customer, or failed to secure one, asks this question. Most people presume that customers want a quality product delivered at a fair rate. Of course, that is true. But customers, whether they inform you so or not, also consider many other factors when choosing their vendors.

The following list explains the major factors customers take into account in their decisions. Different factors are important to different customers.

○ *Availability and attention.* A vendor who is unavailable to customers does not have to worry about being unavailable for very long. If she is unavailable for enough time, customers will leave, and sooner or later she will become available again! Simple, right? Generally speaking, the amount of attention you render your customer can make or break relationships.

○ *Background in the customer's industry.* Many customers believe that their industry is fantastically complex and breathtakingly diverse, when in reality their business may be straightforward and simple. Because these people are technicians in their fields and not necessarily experts in your field, many view their industries as unique and believe that only an experienced professional can effectively manage the work. A plumber does not want to hear about your experience with subcontractors; he wants to know about your experience with plumbers.

Customers rarely understand the concept that experience in any industry broadens your scope, deepens your quality, and enhances your ability to confront different problems and come up with specific, thoughtful solutions.

○ *Communication.* An exceptional salesperson claims that if you have excellent communication with your customers, you will not have to worry about any other factor on this list. He claims that the vast majority of businesspersons neglect communication with their customers, and that it is this fact, more than any other, that is responsible for distancing customers from their sellers.

Who initiates communication in your customer-manager relationship, you or the customer? Do you call your customers to chat? Are you comfortable making the first move?

○ *Confidence.* Customers need to feel the peace of mind that comes with a competent vendor. They want to know that the vendor they have engaged is equal to the task. When you are confident, a customer relies on you both as general business counsel and, over time, as personal counsel. It takes time to build this kind of trust, as vendors become knowledgeable about their customers' personal affairs.

Service providers who realize there is no end to selling a customer usually build the greatest confidence in their customers. Their work is confident, and their counsel is confident. They exude self-confidence even if they secretly feel unconfident.

○ *Followup.* Customers want you to follow through with your ideas and solutions. They often interpret your level of followup as a measure of how important you consider them. Excellent followup means meeting deadlines and keeping promises.

○ *Future orientation.* Traditionally, salespeople have approached their work from a fulfillment point of view. They generally feel more comfortable filling orders. But this myopic view often frustrates customers, who ordinarily value the experience of someone who can apply his or her business skills to a customer's future problems and opportunities.

○ *Location.* Some customers consider the location of their vendors to be extremely important. This is especially true of those who live in small towns and other provincial areas.

Here is an example of two vendors that take advantage of their locations. The first is located just inside the border between a suburb and a large city. This vendor has an address that is just inside the suburb, and the practitioner tells me that he has virtually all the business inside the town, claiming that local townspeople do not want to use big-city salespeople. He also has a significant amount of customers in the big city. The second company moved its office from an expensive, opulent address in an affluent town to a less affluent, adjacent town, to reduce rent expenditure. That practitioner still retains the old town on his letterhead to maintain the illusion that he still does business in the affluent town.

○ *Low fees.* Some customers actually seek the lowest price possible. Every year or several years, they may bid out their work. Obviously, this is not the kind of customer most businesspersons desire.

Pricing is the most misleading item on this list. Almost always, when a customer does change firms, it claims that the reason is price, knowing that this is the one issue his former provider will not challenge. Nine times out of ten, a customer changes service firms for one or more of the other reasons on this list.

○ *Innovation.* As discussed, innovative ideas are usually unexpected by customers. They do not need or expect you to come up with new ideas, but if you do, it is all gravy to them, and they will value your expertise that much more. This usually applies to financial matters, but goes for general business and personal matters as well.

o *Personal contact.* Every customer wants to speak to one person: the manager. Some customers are happy with constant, close personal contact with the manager on a regular basis. Take the time to contact customers. Take them out to lunch; have regular meetings with them. Send Christmas, birthday, and business anniversary cards to them.

o *Personal rapport.* Customers, first and foremost, want a vendor they can deal with, someone with whom they can establish and enjoy the right chemistry. They want to deal with a friend. This kind of close, personalized friendship cements the business relationship and creates a positive atmosphere for referrals and information exchange.

o *Prior relationship.* Occasionally, customers will utilize previous ties with or through college classmates, families, social clubs, civic organizations, or any other group. Establishing social relationships with noncustomers is an excellent foundation for creating future business relationships.

o *Problem solver.* People who can effectively deal with financial, operational, and managerial problems are a gold mine for customers. Customers want a vendor who will not only solve problems, but will also prevent problems. Concentrate on preventative medicine.

o *Quality.* Obviously, every customer wants a high level of quality. Their single greatest difficulty lies in trying to gauge the quality level of a prospective service provider. As with any new relationship, you do not really know what the other party is like until after the relationship has commenced.

o *Range of products and services.* When customers purchase your services, they are seeking a solution to a specific problem. What makes this solution into a long-term relationship is the dynamic nature of business, which means that customers require a range of services. The more services you can offer a prospective customer, the more likely you are to retain established customers, and the more likely it is that your firm can reach new markets. Oddly, many (if not most) customers are unaware of the full range of products and services their vendors provide.

○ *Recommendations.* Trust is the greatest roadblock a vendor faces when attempting to engage a new customer. If the contact does not believe that you can perform as you claim, you have no chance of signing that contact. Customers may feel that trusted influencers can judge the quality of a vendor more easily than the customer itself can. It pays to be close to other financial professionals.

  Recommendations come through a variety of influencers, including professionals, alumni, vendors, customers, friends, and virtually anyone else the customer trusts.

○ *Reputation.* Remember the phrase, "No one ever got fired for buying IBM"? Many prospective customers, especially those who are establishing themselves, want a "name" vendor, to bring prestige and credibility in the eyes of their shareholders, bankers, potential investors, friends, and the press. In short, some customers do not feel comfortable unless they have a widely recognizable service provider.

  Reputation is important for retaining customers. Because of its impact on your reputation, your overall information-gathering effort will have as much to do with retaining customers as it does with getting new ones. All customers like their vendor to be the visible firm in town. It validates their choice.

○ *Value for fees.* Not to be confused with low fees, value plays a significant role in the customer's decision process. Estimates vary, but prospective customers usually accept the lowest bid in anywhere from 40 to 60 percent of new engagement situations. Like many of us, customers like to feel that they received value in excess of the fees.

How Important Are These Qualities?

Every customer you have has engaged you because of your own unique combination of these qualities. When a company seeks out a new vendor, it studies the qualities found on this list. You must exhibit these qualities if you are to successfully secure and retain new customers. Improvement in your rate of developing new business directly reflects your success in revealing these qualities to potential customers or referral sources.

Use this list of qualities for your communication with your customers, prospective customers, and information sources. These qualities should be demonstrated in every customer communication your firm produces. They should inhere in your brochures, your speeches, your sales presentations, and your social conversations. Anything you do, write, or say must effectively communicate your firm's emphasis on these qualities. Review the list regularly to check your progress.

Many sellers feel they must choose between quality and profitability. Your twin goals of profitability and excellent customer service are not mutually exclusive! You will experience higher profitability through excellent customer service.

Learn Leverage

One very successful vendor gives the same advice to every manager. He tells the managers that his first large customer came to him because he invested the relationship with extra knowledge. He spent about 20 hours securing the customer, and gave a lot of value in the information arena.

Why Customers Switch Vendors

Why do customers switch vendors? As mentioned several times, it is rarely because of a major problem. More likely, customers make the switch because of a buildup of numerous small, service-related problems, including:

- Offering anything other than exceptional quality
- Missing schedules and deadlines
- Failing to keep promises
- Poor followup
- Poor communication, either with the client or its employees
- Poor knowledge of the client's business and industry
- Minimal efforts to contact customers
- Frequent employee turnover

Excellent service to existing customers is the fundamental key to gathering information. Excellent service means adding value to your customer's business.

Levels of Value

There are three levels of value inherent in information, data, and opinions. Each value level has its own characteristics.

1. *Generic.* A poor or mediocre item or service that fulfills the barest or most basic need, regardless of expectations. Most unhappy customers, and a surprisingly high number of satisfied customers, get this level of service.
2. *Expected.* An item or service that adequately fulfills consumers' expectations. The level of quality normally separates an expected product from a generic product. This level produces satisfied customers, and although satisfied customers are rarely in a position to refer business to you, they can provide information with sufficient motivation.
3. *Augmented.* An item or service of high quality that is augmented by superb service and supporting products. The main difference between an expected product and an augmented product is the preference of sophisticated customers. This level produces ecstatic customers who actively assist you by referring business to your firm.

Few vendors reach the augmented product stage. Most people who reach this stage are quickly overwhelmed with new business. As the customer load increases, the firm cannot continually produce the high level of service that customers have come to expect, and the firm slips into producing merely good work. But this is the level where relationships become the closest, where trust gets developed, and where the best intelligence is shared.

Growth and Service Problems

It can be difficult to maintain an augmented service level, but it should be a necessary component of your information-gathering program. If your service to existing customers becomes substandard, your information-gathering program is certain to backfire. It will not just stagnate, it will actively decline, and your hard-earned reputation will suffer fastest of all.

Ensuring Excellent Service

Personal service is the reason customers come and go. They want it and expect it. They expect the service from *you*—not your employees, but *you*. They want to know they have access to the person in charge. This trend is particularly apparent with companies that use very large vendors.

Take a sincere interest in customers, beyond their ability to pay your fees. This will ensure that they open up. The easiest way to do this is to put yourself in their shoes, using their personal styles of thinking. Listen to the customers. Do not argue with them, and do not force your own opinion on the customer.

Reply promptly to customer inquiries. Take every phone call, whenever possible, especially the negative calls. In fact, take care of the negative calls first and foremost. If it is a big customer, handle the complaint. Refrain from arguing with an angry customer; he needs time to blow off steam. Sympathize with him. Try not to screen these calls, and be certain to return all phone calls that you cannot take immediately. But above all, learn from the interchange. Find out why the customer was unhappy.

You and your senior management already know the names of your clients' decision makers. Get to know the names of the principals' offspring who work in the business. Acquaint yourself with as many of their decision makers as possible. These employees move around. They may start their own companies, buy out the customer company, or take an influential position in the accounting staff of another company. At any rate, let them remember you positively when they are in a position to solicit bids on proposals.

Try to maintain consistency. As you grow, do not change the fundamental values and quality service that brought you your present customer base. Your consistency provides comfort for your customers and assists you in maintaining excellent customer service.

Try to minimize annoying employee turnover, and delegate more work to the staff, especially when growth necessitates it. Teach your staff to derive information and conclusions from employee turnover. It is important to add people as your firm grows, but remember: Every new person has a different idea of what customer service means, so you will need to teach new employees your firm's philosophy. Develop and implement customer interaction procedures through training.

COMMUNICATION

Many people, consciously or unconsciously, prefer to maintain some distance and difference between themselves and their customers. They like to think that wearing three-piece suits and using jargon with a manufacturing customer impresses the customer with their knowledge. Often, they are merely insecure, or uncomfortable with their differences, and seek solace in arrogantly emphasizing their perceived superiority.

Do not underrate the importance of the manner in which you communicate with your customers. Your dress, your carriage, your manner of speech, your language, even the type of automobile you drive can matter greatly to your customer, prospective customer, or referral source.

I once contacted a large machine shop that built commercial prototypes in an industrial area. I had spent four months working to get the lead, and we were eager to add this customer to our machine shop specialty. The customer needed a full raft of services, and the owners were seeking to change auditors.

The managing partner of our firm attended an initial meeting with the owner of the company. He had never met the owners of the company before, but they hit it off immediately. The manager knew most of the people in the industry, but more important, he communicated well with the owners. He spoke their jargon; during a tour of the factory floor, he showed that he was familiar with the various machines and their functions, and he was able to comment intelligently on their value to the company. In short order, this company became a customer.

As noted, communication is the area in which most people are found wanting. Excellent communication builds your practice. Try these tips:

- *Continuous communication.* Be aware of customer concerns and incorporate them into that customer's own unique service plan. Your internal communication must work well so that affected parties will be open with each other.

- *Be responsive, especially in negative situations.* Understand and respond to customer priorities and deadlines. Return their calls, and solicit and act on their feedback.

- *Your staff must be sensitive to customer needs.* Junior employees spend the most time in front of customers, so it is critical that they realize the importance of attention to customer needs. Have the staff review files and correspondence to know and understand the customers.

- *Review as much work as possible with a customer.* This establishes your concern for her well-being. Concern for the customer builds an emotional base that helps sustain the relationship during difficult periods and strengthens the customer-service provider bond.

○ *Pay attention to any information that may directly affect your customers.* Be aware of industry information, articles, bulletins, or anything else that could concern a particular customer. Make certain that you send the customer a copy.

○ *Develop new information during all customer contacts.* One excellent reason to do client entrance and exit interviews yourself is that it is an ideal time to develop new business. Wangle promises out of customers during the interviews. If a customer makes a vague reference to additional services, secure a date to present him with the benefits of the service. If he makes a tentative promise, schedule a time to discuss it. The key to success is to let the customer know that you are aware of his concerns.

These ideas are all important, but the most important facet of communication is *listening to your customers.* Every businessperson knows that a customer-oriented company is much more likely than a technically oriented firm to retain customers, but few businesspersons really know why this is so. It is true for one reason, and one reason only: Customer-oriented businesses listen to their customers.

Every businessperson thinks she listens to her customers. Every businessperson would like to think she has a firm handle on the desires and needs of her customers. But in actuality, this is far from true. If it were true, no customer would ever leave its vendor; 1 customer out of 12 would not be unhappy with its service provider; information gathering would be moot; and this book would be unnecessary.

Given that listening to customers should be a priority for all businesspersons, let's examine how businesspersons typically listen to their customers. Generally, managers interact with their customers on an ad hoc basis, conversing on issues as they arise.

They judge customer moods when they talk to the clients on the phone and in person, see them at social and civic functions, and discuss their business situations. They greet clients pleasantly and then estimate the customer's mood according to his or her statements and actions.

How well does this observational, reactionary system work? It works fine if you deal with a customer who wears his emotions on his sleeve. If, however, you are dealing with one of the vast majority of clients who prefer to keep their thoughts and motivations private, it falls short.

Most customers tend to keep thoughts of switching vendors to themselves. Out of more than 1,000 prospective customers that considered switching vendors, fewer than 50 informed me that their vendor was aware of the true problems in the relationship.

There are five inherent problems with the observe-and-react system:

1. Although interacting with customers on a day-to-day basis gives a vendor an excellent view into a customer's situation, it allows only a mere glance at the client's surface feelings and almost totally precludes insight into the customer's long-term thoughts, motivations, and concerns. A customer will certainly not give a vendor a critique of his performance if the vendor is performing acceptably. Customers are highly unlikely to give their vendors day-to-day summaries of their feelings about the services they are receiving.

2. As your customer base grows, you experience the distance syndrome, a paradox that afflicts rapidly growing companies. As the firm adds more customers, the amount of time each employee spends with each individual customer decreases. Consequently, each manager experiences less input with which to gauge the thoughts, feelings, and concerns of his customers. Unfortunately, this is the time when your firm will begin to have

infrastructural problems, and your quality of customer service tends to lessen. So, at a time when listening to each customer is becoming even more critical, successful vendors have less time in which to do it!

3. It is difficult enough to uncover a customer's feelings about you. It is virtually impossible to keep track of her feelings about your managers, employees, clerical department, and other aspects of your company.

4. Customers are more sophisticated than in the past. They realize that there is an abundance of quality vendors in the market, and they do not have to rely on a sole source of accounting services anymore.

5. Possibly most important, more and more businesses are actively gathering information. Although a slightly dissatisfied or mildly satisfied customer rarely seeks new accounting help on its own, it may be open to aggressive attention from another suitor.

As businesses grow, personal attention to their established customers can slip. You must keep in contact with your customers. However, if you should have trouble with some of your established customers, you know there has been a mishap in your customer information flow. To rectify customer information inadequacies, it is strongly recommended that public businesses (especially rapidly growing companies) consider customer surveys.

SURVEYS

Virtually every company suffers from a lack of customer information, and the larger the company, the greater the lack. Customer surveys offer the perfect remedy for insufficient customer information. They are sophisticated, comprehensive, and can have a focus as far-ranging or as narrow as you like. They can be general or completely tailored to fit your needs. Anonymous surveys encourage candid comments from customers, who tend to suppress unpleasant remarks in front of their service persons. Surveys are cost-effective; equally important, they prove to customers that you care about their opinions and that you are eager to meet their needs and desires.

Why, then, do so many businesspersons dislike customer surveys? Let's examine several customer survey misconceptions:

- *"We already know our customers well. A survey can't tell us anything."* Have you ever had a customer leave unexpectedly? Surveys will not only tell you in which areas you fall short, but also reveal areas in which your firm could stand to improve—areas that you may be blind to. Surveys can also comment on your managers, staff, and clerical department. They are excellent for identifying blind spots. In fact, this is an underlying reason why many businesspersons actually dislike surveys: consciously or unconsciously, they are afraid of what they will find! Customer surveys are excellent tools for uncovering unhappy customers, because very few customers inform their vendors that they are seeking alternative services.

  If nothing else, a survey will act as an insurance policy, proving that you do indeed have perfect knowledge of your customers.

- *"No one is ever candid in these things."* Some customers are not candid. Most are candid. Your customers will certainly be more candid when they can remain anonymous than when they are speaking with you face to face. Also, surveys expose small problems that are rarely discussed: bills that are too high, phone calls that are not returned, delays, or other minor frustrations.

- *"A survey will annoy my customers and result in negative comments."* Surveys do not annoy customers so much as they annoy vendors who are afraid of what they will read. Surveys convey your concern for the customer to the customer. Yes, your survey responses may have negative comments; they address areas that you need to review.

○ *"Our customers don't have time to fill out a survey."* Although you will not receive a 100-percent return on your survey, enough customers will respond to make it worthwhile. One thing is almost certain: An unhappy customer will fill out a survey and return it to you. Some market researchers feel that the level of returned surveys actually reflects the quality of your firm; that a high number of returns indicates an unhappy customer base. This is not necessarily true, but it would certainly be hazardous to your firm's health to ignore survey comments.

○ *"Surveys cost too much."* Surveys do not have to be expensive. They can be as inexpensive as an additional sheet or two in the monthly billing statement. One firm sends a single-sheet survey with every billing statement, to keep up with customer opinion on a monthly basis.

What can surveys do? What do they accomplish? They can reveal areas in which your firm falls short, for individual customers, individual employees, or in a broad area. Surveys can provide you with the opportunity to improve the very shortcomings that could erode your customer relationships. They are excellent tools for revealing customer perceptions.

When and How to Conduct a Survey

Take care not to distribute surveys during a time of turmoil for your company. If you are having obvious difficulty in a certain area, you do not need a survey to address the problem. Surveys are best for uncovering hidden problems, not emphasizing existing ones. Also, every customer that returns the survey will think long and hard about your firm. Surveys tend to be critical; respondents focus on identifying those areas needing change, not on congratulations for a job well done (customers will do that in person).

How often does your firm arrange collective, comprehensive feedback from your customers? Analyze the frequency with which your firm solicits customer views on their satisfaction levels, the services they currently use, and their image of your firm. If this is your first survey, take the following steps:

○ *Decide on your survey goals.* For your first survey, you may wish to attempt an all-encompassing survey that asks for customer opinions in all areas. In subsequent surveys, you can have a narrower focus.

You may have a specific goal in mind for your survey. Is it to be a manager review? To gauge customer knowledge of your range of services? To announce a new office? To review feelings on a merger or purchase? To review the quality level of staff? Remember the purpose of the survey: it is to assist you in uncovering areas that need improvement.

○ *Announce to your customers that your firm is sponsoring a survey.* Let them know it is coming, and why you are sponsoring the survey ("because we want to continually improve customer service, and we are requesting your input," is a good, candid reason). Explain the scope of the survey, note whether or not it is anonymous, and reiterate your sincere desire to provide customers with better service. If it is a written survey, enclose a self-addressed, stamped envelope.

○ *Assemble the survey questionnaire.* Take care to avoid leading questions on the survey. Questions and requests must be as neutral as possible. Offer the customer the possibility of answers in shades of gray by avoiding true/false questions. Have multiple-choice questions regarding all major areas of the practice, with a final "Comments" section for them to expand on any answers.

Be certain the survey is anonymous, and attach a cover letter explaining the purpose of the survey.

The survey should be short and easy to complete. The length of your survey will have an inverse relationship to the length of the customer responses. The following sample shows some suggested areas to cover:

PLEASE COMMENT ON OUR EMPLOYEES:

- Competence of employees
- Availability of employees
- Inquiry response time
- Issue resolving time
- Satisfaction with representation before auditing personnel
- What do you like best?
- What do you like least?

PLEASE RATE our employees from 1 to 10, with 10 being highest:

Employee Name: _____

    Professional: _____

    Likable: _____

    Caring: _____

    Creative solutions: _____

    Business advice: _____

    Confidentiality: _____

    Aggressiveness: _____

    Quality: _____

    Timeliness: _____

    Rarely makes mistakes: _____

    Frequency of contact: _____

    Communication: _____

    Service: _____

    Phone followup: _____

    Quality: _____

    Problem solving: _____

    Availability: _____

What do you like best?

Ask customers to review your staff on communication, service, followup, quality, problem solving, and availability (at least). Ask what customers like best and what they like least. Ask them about expectations.

- *Distribute the survey to your customers.* Mail all the surveys simultaneously. Have one person assemble all answers.
- *Carefully consider every answer.* When you compile the results, do not dismiss any of the information brought to light, even if it is in an area of common complaint, like fees.

   Do not generalize. You may see one solitary, unique answer among a horde of other responses. Consider it. If it rings true, address the issue.
- *Make changes in the areas identified by the survey.* This is the most important part of any survey. As with an employee survey, do not whitewash problems: do not ignore them and do not rationalize them. Unaddressed difficulties, whether identified from customer or employee surveys, only emphasize problems. If you are unprepared to institute changes, it would do more harm than good to run a survey.

Responses

What kind of responses can you expect? Well, let's review a few:

- *The worst thing your customers can tell you.* "Everything's fine" or any other very brief answer. Though it may be a personality issue, it's important for you to realize that a client's uncommunicativeness is an initial signal that all may not be well.
- *The best thing your customers can tell you.* "I'm unhappy." At least they are communicating. At least they are coming to you. They are offering you direct information that is very personal.
- *The worst thing a prospect can tell you.* "I just changed vendors." Unless it's your first-ever contact with the prospect, this tells you that your information-gathering apparatus is in serious need of repair.
- *The best thing a prospect can tell you.* "I'm happy with my current firm . . . I'm just unhappy in a couple of areas." This is

the best information you can receive. It tells you that the prospect is not necessarily happy *and* that he or she is willing to share that information with you.

EXIT INTERVIEWS

Many people think that interviewing customers who are leaving the firm is useless. Why waste the time? If a customer has departed, the standard reaction is to rationalize the reason for the departure and deny any firm or manager shortcomings. When customers leave, managers usually sigh at the former customer's obvious lack of appreciation for their efforts, and turn their attention to other matters.

The attitude that it is always the customer who is in the wrong when a customer leaves is pervasive throughout professional industries. The typical manager becomes defensive during a reading of exit interview notes, and passionately defends himself and his firm against the former customer's criticisms. But the fact of the matter is that many people are blind when it comes to their own shortcomings. It is difficult for a businessperson to actually listen to negative comments. This self-imposed blindness to reality prevents businesspersons from recognizing areas that may require change.

An exit interview is an excellent opportunity to gauge your shortcomings. Yes, customers leave for irrational reasons, or because they feel that expenses or fees are too high, but they often leave because of difficulties of which your management is unaware. Because of the potential benefits, you should always hold exit interviews with departing customers, no matter how obvious their reasons for leaving. There are almost always underlying reasons besides those cited by the unhappy customers, particularly when they have had significant interaction with firm employees or management. These underlying reasons will reveal potential difficulties in the firm.

Because of the rancor sometimes involved, former customers often do not inform their vendors of the exact reason for their dissatisfaction. Though a customer generally states a reason for leaving, she rarely allows insight into her true thoughts, because of the close nature of the relationship. Therefore, the exit interview must be conducted by someone who is distanced from your firm. Other possible interviewers may include someone from marketing, the firm administrator, or an external consultant. This helps to draw candid comments from the former customer. If you feel it necessary, assure the customer that her name will be kept confidential, and that only her specific concerns will be revealed to the manager.

Wait for one month after the customer leaves to interview the former customer. This way, possibly angry customers should have cooled down, and will be more likely to give candid answers.

The interviewer should present himself, if possible, as a firm administrator who merely desires to find out why, how, where, and when your firm fell short. Because former customers do not wish to step on toes, they will rarely mention names during exit interviews. However, because of the nature of the conversation, "who" fell short will become obvious, and changes can and should be implemented by the managing manager to remedy the problem.

There are a few ground rules for the interview. First, remember that the more positive and more sympathetic you are to the ex-customer, the better you leave him feeling toward you and your firm, and the more likely he is to be candid with you. With this final, assuaging treatment, the ex-customer will be less likely to create ill will and more likely to return as a customer.

When conducting the interview, use open-ended questions. Closed-ended questions require a brief, yes-or-no response: "So, were we too expensive?" "Uh . . . yes." The only time you should get down to specifics is when the former customer brings up specific issues; then you zero in on those issues. Finally, make certain the customer knows you appreciate his past business, that you are disappointed that he has left, and that you would welcome the opportunity to serve him again.

If your company engages in telemarketing, a telemarketer may run across former customers. You may use a telemarketer to perform an impromptu exit interview. Customers that leave may often return, and an exit interview is a perfect opportunity to effect that change.

ENTRY INTERVIEWS

A similar service should be extended to new customers. You should overservice the customer during the first six months, or until just after completion of the first significant service to the new customer (whichever is longer). Call the customer immediately after you have performed the work, and solicit its response. Adjust accordingly.

Listening to your customers will yield superb dividends. By actively listening to their concerns, by concentrating on hearing what they are telling you, you will become a valued counselor and a trusted confidante. This level of trust is necessary to progress to the next level: customers as information sources.

INFORMATION SOURCES

It is important to have an impressive customer list for more reasons than building your ego. Customers are your key to the future. Firms typically receive at least 50 percent of all new business from their current customers. Your best customers will make the best referrals, as people listen to key customers, but do not ordinarily pay attention to transitory or marginal customers.

Your customers should be your best and most important information sources. Show them that you care about them. Send them copies of articles that will interest them, along with mailers and newsletters. Spend time developing and selling new services to your customers. Brainstorm with your staff (especially managers) to produce new service ideas to pursue with your customers. If you are offering a new service, contact your customers and potential customers.

The most crucial time in a new relationship is during the first six months, for two reasons. First, the customer wants confirmation that it has made the right decision. Secondly, if anyone has referred this customer to you, the referral source is sure to speak to the new customer during that six-month period and ask how the new relationship is working out. How would you like your new customer to answer?

(a) "Terrible. I can't believe you referred the guy to me. He never calls, I get dinged for a bill every time I pick up the phone, and I'm getting terrible service."

(b) "Okay. Not great, not terrible. Wish he was more responsive."

(c) "Pretty good. About what I expected."

(d) "Fabulous. He's the best thing that ever happened to me, and frankly, I owe you for recommending this guy. Where did you ever find him?"

Which opinion do your customers have? Is it the last one, (d)?

Which of These Levels of Satisfaction Produces References and Intelligence?

The customers in the latter group will clearly provide the most and best market intelligence to you. The relationship will be closest, the trust will be highest, and the customer will most likely feel that an information exchange is of mutual benefit. Less and less intelligence can be expected with each declining level, though (as discussed in the preceding section) the most intelligence is required from unhappy customers.

Actually, every one of those opinions produces referrals. Opinions (a) and (d) produce active referrals; these customers will give you a negative or positive referral without being asked. Opinions (b) and (c) produce passive referrals; these customers will not say anything about your firm unless they are asked.

Customers are either dissatisfied, satisfied, or ecstatic. If they are dissatisfied, you can be certain that their close friends will know about it, their banker and attorney will know about it, and they will waste no time telling anyone who asks which company *not* to consider. A poor reputation spreads wildly among service-oriented firms.

If your customer is merely satisfied (e.g., 75 to 85 percent of all customers), then the relationship is acceptable. This is the ideal situation for many people. If someone asks your customer if she knows of a good vendor, she should recommend you. Otherwise, these customers rarely think about you.

When you perform at such a high level that your customers are ecstatic with you and your work, they will actively channel opportunities your way. Your excellent service and communication will propel your customers' estimation of you upward, and reward you with greater market intelligence.

If My Customers Are Satisfied, Why Don't I Get Referrals and Market Intelligence?

Most of your customers think four things. First, that you are the greatest vendor available. Second, as a great performer, you must be swamped with work. Third, because you are swamped with work, you must have as much business as you need. Finally, they think you share a more or less common degree of knowledge . . . until you ask. You need to let customers know that you are not overworked and would appreciate market intelligence, new business, and referrals.

There was a large, regional, midwestern consulting firm that hit a scarce information-gathering period after a five-year growth spurt. After eight months of silence from the market, the managing partner enlisted the help of a information-gathering consultant to help shake the firm out of its development doldrums. The consultant initially asked about the level of market intelligence referred by existing customers. The answer was unanimous: little intelligence had been delivered by current customers during the previous year. Puzzled, the consultant asked the managers whether they were asking their customers for new business. Each manager said yes.

The information-gathering consultant surveyed a cross-section of the managers' customers, suspecting that there were service-related problems that prevented customers from delivering intelligence to the managers. Instead, he found a number of satisfied customers—virtually all of which were unaware that the firm was seeking market information!

Attitude

A salesperson once insisted to me that people in his business were considered to be less than completely desirable by customers. He had none of the flash that seems like such a prerequisite for salespeople, yet he literally had 50 percent more customers and 100 percent more revenue than the next most productive salesperson at his firm, and his average annual revenue was considerably higher than that of salespeople in typical international businesses. I asked him why he felt that way.

"It's all attitude," he responded. "You see, the average salesman views himself as the savior of his customers. That is, he is providing a product necessary to a segment of the population that not only desperately needs his product, but *wants* it as well.

"That is where the difficulty lies with salespeople. Every salesman has an ego that tells him he's the professional; that he is directing his customer's future, and that every customer should listen to what he says. Every salesman feels that every one of his customers desperately needs him.

"But as salesmen get older, their memories can get selective. They forget who is paying the bills. They forget that customers are good salesmen in their own right. They forget that the customer, or the prospective customer, has his own set of priorities and his own set of emotional needs. This attitude on the part of salespeople has led to a certain unsavory reputation. While the businessmen view themselves as saviors of their customers, they view salespeople as parasites. And, to a certain extent, this is true.

"Businessmen see salespeople as an annoying but necessary part of their business, and the sad truth is they prefer to use us as little as possible. Have you ever heard a businessman say he wants to increase commissions? Of course not, and you never will. Customers need salespeople and they need your advice, but they hate having to pay for it.

"How do you change this? Well, you never truly can. But you can mitigate it by presenting yourself as a consultant to them in their business, someone who takes care of them. For example, I never give customers advice by saying, 'You ought to do this,' or 'I recommend that you do that.' I say, 'Mike, this is what *we* want to do . . .' With this approach, customers appreciate your value that much more. Our appreciation of our customers should be demonstrated in our attitude toward our customers."

CUSTOMER BASE

Terminating Existing Customers: One Step Back, Two Steps Forward

One of your largest customers, worth $5,000,000 in annual revenue, is a computer memory board manufacturer who is giving you problems. Though he always pays his bills, he is now just past 120 days late with the final installment. Earlier this year, he ignored your advice not to get involved in a supplier relationship, and is now experiencing shortages. A few minutes ago, you got off the phone with a trusted manager who thinks she has uncovered evidence that the customer is skimming cash from his company. You sigh as you contemplate your options.

What do you do? Many businesses would swallow their anger, frustration, and disappointment (not to mention pride and common sense); after all, $500,000 in lost revenue is nothing to sneeze at. You may be uncertain as to how, or even whether, you could make up the lost revenue in the near future. With crossed fingers, you decide to keep the customer on your customer base and try once again to convert him into an ideal customer. You hope you are making the right decision.

As your company grows, there should come a time when you cannot service your smaller or less appealing customers profitably. At that point, furthering the relationship is counterproductive for both parties, and it is necessary to terminate the relationship. When it is time for an amicable split, the company refers the customer to a smaller firm more suited to the customer. Most firms and customers recognize the necessity of the move, and it is rarely debated.

Ask yourself the final question: Does this customer deliver business intelligence to me? Do we have anything beyond a customer-vendor relationship? Is this client adding to my market knowledge base?

The Ideal Customer

Let's review what we want from an ideal customer. We want profitability and challenging work, of course; we also want honesty, cooperation, and acceptance of our advice. We expect them to pay on time and agree to reasonable cost increases. Finally, we want to share market intelligence with them. Ideal customers work within these parameters and rarely cause you or your firm difficulty. Their consistency benefits the entire firm and assures your growth.

Marginal Customers

This being the real world, we all have customers with whom we have, to put it charitably, less than ideal relationships. Customers who do not accept advice, consistently pay late, or who are dishonest and uncooperative are the bane of any businessperson's existence. Unfortunately, they are endemic to the industry; every firm has its lower-echelon customers.

Most businesspersons are loath to terminate relationships unless they are pushed over the brink. Perhaps they are afraid to lose the revenue; perhaps they are afraid of the negative publicity of the break; perhaps they simply value the relationship with the customer.

We are all aware of businesses that struggle at the existence level, which are proud that they have never voluntarily released a customer and always fight it when customers leave. This attitude has several outcomes. First, one may find oneself in litigation regularly. Second, a great deal of time is wasted with marginal customers. Third, these customers are usually close-mouthed; it is nearly impossible to get information from them. Fourth, troublesome customers tend to demand a disproportionate amount of your time and attention, often for trivial matters. This has the doubly debilitating effect of keeping you from adequately servicing your top-echelon customers and reducing your information-gathering and networking time.

Most companies consider this treatment of lower-echelon customers to be necessary, if for no other reason than to supplement the fees generated from higher-echelon customers. However, your working relationship with all of your customers suffers because of the negative effects from these customers, even if the bad effects are not readily visible. Indeed, lower-echelon customers sap your business development efforts.

Further, you have your future customer base to consider. Poor customers tend to refer other poor customers to you. Conversely, superb customers usually refer other superb customers to you.

Finally, some information sources will hesitate to refer high-quality customers to you if they perceive that you have a substandard customer base. In essence, your customer base reflects your firm's quality to the business community.

Releasing Lower-Echelon Customers

Releasing your low-echelon customers has a number of benefits:

o It opens up your time for information gathering. Information gathering is an activity for which effort is directly proportional to success.

o It frees up your time to work with those customers who desire and deserve your help, and will accordingly treat you with respect.

o It allows you to work fewer hours. Because good customers are more profitable, it extends your leverage and increases your profit margin. This is a variation on the old 80–20 rule: "If you get rid of 20 percent of your customers, you will get rid of 80 percent of your headaches and your profits will rise by 30 percent."

o It actually builds your prestige to release accounts. Your best customers generally have the most favorable opinion of you and your firm, and your marginal customers usually have marginal opinions of you and your firm. The latter become like an anchor, dragging down your hard-won reputation. By releasing these customers, your reputation soars.

o Finally, it is possible to secure additional income via marginal customers. Several businesses release their marginal accounts by selling them to smaller businesses that are eager for growth and are willing to invest more time with marginal customers.

One local company uses a variation on this theme, by either referring or selling its troublesome customers to its closest competitors. It referred one of its low-echelon customers to a crafty local competing businessperson, Joseph, who told me he was well acquainted with the firm's practice of dumping marginal customers. Joseph convinced the customer that it would be better off with the previous vendor, and referred the customer back to the newest salesman at the original vendor!

Decide for yourself which factors are most important to you and grade your customers accordingly.

Mid-Echelon Customers

As discussed, it is best to deal with lower-echelon customers by eliminating them from your customer list. What about mid-level customers? These are a mixed breed, of course. Some of these clients exhibit the potential to become upper-echelon customers. Deal with them by making it clear the type of behavior you expect from customers. Speak with them in person, courteously, and outline the changes you see as necessary to improve your relationship. Listen to your customer's point of view. Be positive, and emphasize how a mutually beneficial relationship is best for both of you, and how a mutual exchange of information can benefit you both.

Customers and Revenue

While strengthening your customer base, you must prepare yourself for the customers that may leave. Do not allow any one customer to be responsible for too much of your revenue base. Frequently tell your upper-echelon clients how much you appreciate their business.

The following collection hints may help you to collect fees more rapidly while still salvaging the customer relationship:

○ *Communicate with the customer.* Good communication with your customer prior to the engagement reduces collection headaches later on. Billing policies should be outlined in the engagement letter. Explain your billing policy to the customer during the initial meeting prior to the engagement.

○ *Train your customers.* I once spoke with an engineer who bragged that he had his lawyer trained. "My lawyer does exactly what I tell him to," he said. "I do not pay him until he brings my completed patent applications over to me. When he brings that statement, I give him a check in full. I've got a great deal." The customer beamed.

Who's training who?

○ *Talk to your customers on a regular basis.* A five-minute phone call every month to your annual-only customers can pay dividends in several ways, including the possibility of referrals and new work for current customers. You can discuss business, the economy, market forces, influencers . . . and you can interact with a customer who may be unhappy with fees. If nothing else, you will cement your relationship. By speaking with your customers on a regular basis, you will find that your outstanding receivables balance will shrink; it is difficult to talk to someone every month while holding out on paying outstanding bills.

COMPETING THROUGH KNOWLEDGE

When the market is saturated with producers, and the product is not easily differentiable, there are only two methods which will appreciably increase sales: lowering price, or emphasizing significant unique product features.

—Peter Drucker

Many people, especially those who have been around for a while, watch the proliferation of competitors with some alarm. While they appreciate that their business and their industry are growing, they realize there is a finite amount of business to be had, with a seemingly bottomless pit of firms opening up to service this business. Although competition tightens continuously, sometimes immediate tougher competition is inevitable, so margins will get squeezed and price increases will be postponed at many firms.

Many people hold the view that competition is good for the profession, but low pricing is not the way to survive. It sure is not the route to prosperity—but as long as there are enough young lions around who can survive on thinner margins (and are tired of being employees anyway), business will be stuck with competition.

In an entrepreneurial atmosphere, many managers are breaking away from their former firms to open their own practices. Many of these newly founded firms, as well as established firms, will lowball price to build their customer bases.

The local office of a national furniture retailer was renowned for its aggressive information-gathering tactics. A junior saleswoman had been in many meetings with various prospective customers, and often drew up proposals with the senior salespeople. I asked her about competing through cost on a national level, and she rolled her eyes, offering the following example:

"Our sales manager and I had just finished reviewing the furnishing needs of a large, local manufacturing concern. We extensively reviewed their facilities and plant, and I estimated the value of the engagement at between $550,000 and $575,000.

"Sitting down, we knew the company owner was impressed with us. He and my sales manager, Dennis, sat across from each other, joking about their golf games, and there was an expectant pause. Dennis smiled and said, 'Roy, we'd love to work together. I figure we can get you shipshape for about $515,000.' My eyes nearly popped out, and I figured the manager had miscalculated badly. This was unusual, because this manager had a reputation for accurate estimates.

"I was even more surprised, however, when the president of the company fixed his gaze on Dennis and said, '[Another international company] will do it for $485,000.'

"I almost got up right then, since the firm would obviously lose money on the job, but my final surprise came when the sales manager didn't bat an eye and said, 'We'll match it.'"

MISINFORMATION

Misinformation refers to the practice of generating false information in the market for the purpose of misdirecting competitors or influencers. Misinformation has been an accepted information-delivery tactic for centuries. It is a very real possibility in any business in which a number of competitors bid for clients. Is it unprofessional? Sometimes. It damages reputations and creates false images. It may lower a firm's prestige and esteem. It can place pressure on staff and engender shoddy work. It can open up the business to creditor and shareholder lawsuits. It may reduce the premium on loyalty and attract cost-conscious customers.

What if You Are the Victim of Misinformation?

What if another businessperson spreads misinformation? Do you panic? Do you offer to cut costs in a knee-jerk fashion? Do you have a "personal chat" with the offending businessperson? Do you do nothing?

Many people panic, give in to their first reaction, and reduce price to retain clients. This is a last resort, not a first resort. If a competitor is spreading misinformation about you or your business, you have a number of options, including:

○ *Preparation.* Remember the Five Ps, or "proper planning prevents poor performance." The military knows that 90 percent of winning a battle lies in proper preparation. As mentioned repeatedly throughout this section, it is easier to save the customer if the relationship is solid to begin with. This means regular, periodic interaction with your customer; tracking the customer's information and intelligence and making certain that it aligns with your own; offering advice without being asked for it; steering the customer away from potential future difficulties; remembering your customers' important dates; and ensuring that your staff interacts with your customers as well as you do. With this kind of relationship, it is much less likely that your customer will even talk to another vendor, much less become susceptible to misinformation campaigns.

○ *Get to know your customers' professionals.* Every professional lives off information. Because so many consulting, process, banking, accounting, and legal firms now have compensation programs with bonuses or commissions based on new business, there is more pressure than ever to bring in new business and new market intelligence. If you have a solid relationship with the professionals who work with your customers, it is much less likely that they will refer business away from you, and much more likely that they will share information with you. This is particularly important for small to midsize companies.

One vendor who claims he has never had a customer referred away from him says his secret is to perform free work for his customers' information sources!

○ *Examine your current information-generating structure.* Is there a way you can improve it? Is it delivering misinformation in the first place?

○ *Talk with the customers.* What is bothering them? Why isn't the relationship working? Fees are often used as an excuse by customers who leave businesses. In reality, poor communication, bad service, lack of timeliness, low quality, lack of expertise, or loss of a favored staff businessperson are often the actual reasons a customer leaves the firm.

○ *Don't match the competitor's misinformation.* Do make sure you share the true story with clients, prospects, and influencers. Be very proactive about it.

○ *Don't lowball price.*

○ *Review the competitor's proposal with your customer.* If your customer has been approached with misinformation and a simultaneous sales proposal, you have every right to use every weapon in your own arsenal. It is your customer that has been approached, so you can ask to review the other vendor's proposal. If there are any flaws or differences in the proposal, point them out. If the other businessperson's numbers are just an estimate and not a fixed fee, point that out to the customer and offer a fixed fee of your own. Review the list of pricing and rates, and compare it with your past performances. If they vary, point these out to the customer. If the other vendor has guaranteed pricing for one year, offer to guarantee fees for two years.

- o *Keep in touch.* If all else fails, you still have a relationship with the customer, even if it has been torn away from you. It is important that you call that ex-client on a very regular basis. Keep remembering her on her important dates. Don't pressure her, just be there for her.

- o *If you lose the client, offer to review the other vendor's work.* No one knows the customer as well as you do. Remind her yet again of your lengthy relationship.

Future of Misinformation

What is the future of misinformation? It is certain that misinformation will continue to be used as an across-the-board strategy. While it can be an effective narrow strategy, misinformation is unnecessary, cheapens your image, and will hurt your revenue over time.

CONCLUSION

Although competitors differ on pricing, margins, quality, product mix, employee relations, service, communications levels, and virtually every other aspect of their businesses, it is commonly agreed that the key to success begins with excellent customer relations. It can further be extrapolated that the greatest quantity and quality of market information and intelligence should come from your customers. Quite frankly, superb client relations are the sole advantage some companies have over their competition.

When working with your customers, keep in mind the following:

- o Most clients want consistency above all else. Consistent communication, consistent service, consistent relationships, consistent pricing. If you make any customer relationship effort, begin with consistency.

- o After consistency, delivering value in excess of client expectations is most appreciated by your clients. Clients desire an augmented level of value. Exceptional value will pay two dividends: one literal, one figurative. Certainly, clients are prepared to pay more for value, so profits will rise. Second, your relationship becomes more intimate, and the closer you get to your clients, the higher the value of the market information they can deliver to you.

7

Referral Source Information

The only thing worse than being talked about is not being talked about.

—Oscar Wilde

THE ART OF NETWORKING

On my first job out of college, I was gathering intelligence for my employer and I admittedly didn't know where to begin. Therefore, I sought out the manager in charge of knowledge management (the term didn't exist at the time) at a large, successful, local office of a national firm. I knew he would have nothing to fear from my firm, because we were fairly small at the time. He agreed to meet with me. During a very pleasant lunch conversation, I asked him which activity he would concentrate on if he were starting a new business. He said, "There is only one thing you need to do if you want to start a business. If you want to secure any business, if you want to engage challenging customers, you need to become known. Market recognition is the most important thing a business can have. If no one knows you, you are dead in the water. And if you don't know your market, your industries, your clients, your prospects, and your referral sources, you're dead in the water too."

It is often difficult for prospective customers to evaluate the quality of a particular product or service, and they often settle for evaluating the surrounding aspects. Their most important clue as to the actual quality of the firm comes not from the presentation itself (anyone can be impressive for an hour), but from the advice and/or opinion of a trusted third party. The relationships in your infrastructure will, in large part, determine not only your company's growth, but also your ability to gain intelligence and manage your knowledge base. Thus, creating an extensive referral network is an extremely effective information-gathering method, one that will be directly or indirectly responsible for virtually every customer you secure and retain.

This becomes apparent when a successful business moves to expand its practice: Its first order of business is to promote itself and increase the firm's positive recognition in the business community. Establishing and maintaining an impressive network of information sources should become your singular goal.

Before we established our direct, active information-gathering activities (telemarketing and direct mail programs), fully half of my firm's new knowledge came from existing clients. Another quarter came through acquired clients and the remaining intelligence came from noncustomer information sources.

Building an Information Network

First, Contact Information Sources. You cannot wait for information sources to contact you. No matter how visible you are, if you don't expose yourself, at least to a small extent, to the right people, you will never hear from them. There are certain influential people in every town and in every industry, and these people can be potent information generators for you. Research and identify the people who are prominent power wielders and decision makers in your local community and industry specialties and plan the most effective means to approach and impress them.

Not surprisingly, these people are difficult to contact. It is not their nature to flash a neon sign advertising their influence. Like most powerful people, they are secure in the knowledge that people will seek *them* out. Here again, you need to be alert for opportunities to meet these people. Your reference list should include customers, friends, professionals, heads of industry associations, and local politicians. Pay attention to people who are important in the business community infrastructure. Develop relationships with them, and you can create knowledge networks with them. Solicit their opinions and advice. Form strategic relationships with them.

Cultivate Knowledge Sources through Regular Contact. A single meeting or conversation is insufficient for potential knowledge sources to remember you positively. Periodic mail reminders (newsletters and various fliers) and phone calls are effective means of cultivating recognition while generating sales opportunities. Visit their places of business. Call them. Take them out to lunch, dinner, a ball game, or a golf match; invite them to your speeches; send them your newsletters. Ask them if you can display your literature with theirs.

Though correspondence is effective and is simple to use, it is not as effective as a phone contact, just as a phone contact is not as effective as an in-person contact. Of course, it is impossible to contact all your information sources within a brief time span, so a coordinated program of mailings and personal contacts is essential for maintaining relationships with your network. Establish a mixed contact schedule of mailings, phone contacts, social events, and business meetings. Ideally, you should maintain a separate tickler file for your normal appointments, your contact contacts, and your referral source contacts. Do not go longer than three months between most contacts, and absolutely no longer than six months between any type of contact. A sample calendar is shown in Exhibit 7.1.

Exhibit 7.1   Sample Calendar

	CUSTOMER	REFERRAL/REFERENCE SOURCE
January	QTRLY REV	MAIL ANNUAL TAX PLANNING GUIDES
February	TAX APPT	LUNCH
March	YEAR END MTG	NEWSLETTER
April	QTRLY REV	GOLF
May	LUNCH	LUNCH
June	NEWSLETTER	CHARITY VOLLEYBALL TOURNEY
July	QTRLY REV	BALL GAME
August	LUNCH	LUNCH
September	NEWSLETTER	NEWSLETTER
October	QTRLY REV	INFLUENCER
November	MAIL HOLIDAY CARDS	
December	HOLIDAY OPEN HOUSE/NEWSLETTER	

The best way to cultivate good sources is to educate them about your firm's strengths and breadth of services. Essentially, you are training an outside salesperson who is positively predisposed to sharing information with you and your firm.

By paying attention to the people in the infrastructure, you direct their perception of your firm, and influence not just how they will refer your services to others but also how frequently they will share information and what kind of information they give you. Don't just promise to share information with them (a tit-for-tat arrangement is ultimately a dead end); form strategic relationships with them. Vendors, suppliers, customers, prospects, influencers, and others can all help you.

Get Them on Your Side. When gathering intelligence from prospective customers, one is careful to listen to them and help them solve their problems, including the problems that concern their influencers. The same is true for disseminating information to potential information sources. Their concerns are that you perform well for your common customers, that your shared information be of high quality, and that they will benefit from the relationship in other ways as well.

What Is the Best Thing an Influencer Can Tell You?

"No one likes you . . . and hasn't for a while."

I worked with a large professional services firm that was losing big in its markets. No one in-house really knew why, so all 12 shareholders of the business had a closed-door session with one of the most prominent influencers in the community. He laid it on the line:

- o No one had a good opinion of anyone in the firm except for the managing partner and his key salesman.
- o Other firms in the industry had made solid inroads with the influencer community, leaving this firm far behind.
- o Their customers weren't very happy.
- o Their quality was slipshod.

A plain-talking, candid influencer is worth her weight in gold.

What Is the Second-Best Thing an Influencer Can Tell You?

"I've got another lead for you."

Nothing highlights an influencer's confidence in you more than their sharing a lead (or information) with you.

THE RIGHT KNOWLEDGE

Most people have established an influencer network. Few of them utilize it to its fullest extent, though, and fewer still understand how to maximize their referral network benefits.

Organize Your Information Sources

Time is limited. You cannot know everyone in the business community intimately, so you need to maximize your information-gathering time with the most effective contacts. You are no doubt aware that the most attractive influencers are besieged by people who clamor for their attention. Therefore, to be heard above the multitude, your approach must fall on receptive ears. Make a list of your closest information sources, and recognize where they are in the following categories.

Type A Knowledge Sources. These information sources think of you and call you before any other firm, either to exchange information or to make a referral. You work with them, meet with them, share intelligence with them, and refer business to them on a regular basis. These sources are the stronghold of your referral base, and you should treat them accordingly. If the 80–20 rule holds true, you will get 80 percent of your intelligence and contacts from 20 percent of your referral network, so give them 80 percent of your attention.

These sources help you in other ways. Because they are close to you, you can treat them as external business barometers. They are most probably candid with you about your firm and services, your standing in the marketplace, the status of your competition, and other important matters.

If you notice that a close influencer's attention is slipping, have a candid talk with him or her. When we are racing madly to keep up with the marketplace, we can lose sight of ourselves and our firm. Your best outside information sources are often your best sources of constructive criticism. If they offer comments (and you should periodically ask), take their comments seriously.

Type B Information Sources. These sources refer you and other firms simultaneously. They have a positive attitude toward you and hold you in high esteem. However, they share solid relationships with other people as well.

This group offers excellent potential intelligence to you, and it is usually larger than your Type A sources. Spend quality time with Type B sources to upgrade them to Type A status. How? First, if your service quality is below that of other firms in your market niche, improve your quality. This is key to improving any relationship. Secondly, add as many new services or products as possible, and improve the individual, service-related aspects of your practice. Finally, give them plenty of extra attention and maintain consistent personal contact to solidify the relationship.

Type C Influencers. These are the professionals who deal with your customers on a regular basis—but of whom you are not aware. Contacting these professionals commences promising referral and influencer relationships and tightens your current customer relationships.

Early in my career, I arranged a meeting with the senior vice president of a regional office of one of the largest banks in the state. In glowing terms, I spoke of the quality of our firm, our wonderful treatment of our customers, our timeliness, our expertise, and the superb value we extended to our customers. He looked bored, leaned back, and asked, "Tell me the names of some of your customers." His bored look vanished when I mentioned the name of our largest customer. He said, "You know, of course, that company is our single largest customer." (I had no idea.) "Of course you do," he finished. That day he referred me three leads, two of whom became customers worth $20,000 in annual fees.

Type C information sources should prove to be one of your most lucrative sources. Using your customer list as a guide, find out which professionals work with your customers. Delete those who are already in close contact with your firm. Your natural information sources are the professionals who have customers in common with you but do not interact closely with you.

If I could give just one piece of advice to businesspersons, it would be to get to know their customers' professionals by sending those professionals a letter detailing their relationship with the common customer. Then follow up the letter with a meeting.

Type D Information Sources. These are the professional firms that will not refer business to you, but will give you a good recommendation when one is requested. Often, these successful professionals have been in the area for years and realize that a large network of contacts is important. They will share superficial information with you, but are not yet close enough to you to form solid relationships.

These successful professionals are well known in the community, and have probably been referring business to the same firm in the same location for years. These diligent people either know you and your firm well, or they don't know you at all. If they are unfamiliar with you, introduce yourself and let them know who you are and what makes your firm different. Though they will rarely refer business to you, they will give you a positive referral when asked. It is difficult to develop relationships with these people, because it is tantamount to asking them to forgo or break other long-term relationships.

The best opportunity for upgrading Type D information sources is when that source's favorite contact drops out of the marketplace. At that point, there is usually a grace period when the source makes other contacts. This source's individual influence and power alone makes it worthwhile for you to contact him or her at this time.

Type E Information Sources. These are the influencers that are not yet aware of you. Don't make the mistake of believing them to be neutral; indeed, you might as well consider them opponents. Why? Most professionals who are unaware of you will not share intelligence. They most likely will share information with another favorite firm while ignoring you. If someone does not know you, she cannot give you a good reference, because she does not want to chance damaging her reputation if the quality of your work is low. Second, she wants to channel business to her favored reference sources. Third, if a potential customer asks about your firm, she doesn't want to admit she doesn't know you; this would be a subtle failing on her part; implying that she is not as familiar with the professional market as she should be. Consequently, it is much easier for her to comment negatively on you. She retains the confidence of her customer; the customer does not approve you for services; and the professional source refers the customer to her favorite, familiar service firm, thereby cementing the relationships with both her customer and her favorite referral targets.

This is a vast group. Are there exceptions? Absolutely. A subset of this category, which you can later peg to your A or B lists, will be influencers who are new arrivals to the area. As with professionals currently doing business with your customers, new influencers should be natural intelligence sources. These new professionals (especially bankers) are in a business development mode, and tend to encounter more prospective customers than established professionals. But because they don't know anyone yet, they have no established relationships with other service firms, and are ripe for a new relationship.

To establish these relationships, have your secretary canvass the area's commercial banks and update your mailing list every six months. Bankers (and other professionals) are a mobile lot, and you will encounter many people who are new to the industry, the area, or their current firm. Take them to lunch and sell them on your firm!

Type F Information Sources. These are the professional firms that refer business away from you. Perhaps you didn't perform for one of their customers, or they perceive your firm unfavorably, or there is a personality conflict. Whatever the reason, they can damage your reputation. Unfortunately, it is rarely worth the sustained effort it would take to repair this kind of relationship. By all means, make the attempt, but if nothing shows as promising, discontinue the effort immediately.

Your Customers' Information Network of Influencers

As discussed, your customers are your natural information sources. Can you name your customers' professionals: their attorneys, bankers, insurance brokers, business consultants, stock brokers, pension administrators, bonding agents, and factors?

Most businesspersons know only a few of their customers' professionals, and their contact with these people, though constant, is not as regular as it could be. These professionals are your natural information sources. They are the ones who are acquainted with your work and are familiar with your quality. They know you by name and reputation and should already be receiving copies of your collateral e-mails, newsletters, holiday cards, and so on; in fact, any relevant communication that goes out to your customers. They should be invited to your annual functions and your open houses. Particularly important or visible professionals should be invited to sporting events, dinners, free seminars, or other functions.

Your communications with these people should be very clear. These professionals are close enough to you to give you honest feedback instead of gratuitous, back-scratching "advice." Acquaintances and contacts are much less likely to speak of you with any candor. But people with whom you work will give you their referrals, and talk with you about your market and your competition. You already have something in common with these people. Use it!

Alumni and Former Coworkers

Keep in touch with former employees and coworkers, except when the separations were truly unpleasant. You should maintain contact with former alums and friends to maximize the future opportunities they may bring. A former employee or friend can prove to be either an excellent source of referrals and information, or an opponent whose vitriolic diatribes may cause damage.

Ideally, you should keep close to them, maintain contact with them, and share information with them. After all, it's free.

The Unconscious Network

An excellent, final reason to create a referral network is the *unconscious* network. Your conscious network is those information sources with whom you currently interact. Your unconscious network consists of contacts who encounter your service indirectly, whether through your information sources or other sources. Remember that everyone knows about 150 people. You and your firm are affected by what a person says about you, whether or not what he says is accurate.

Meeting and Contacting Information Sources

There are many different places to meet information sources. The following locales are the most common and will lead to other sources.

Membership in Professional Groups, Clubs, Charities, and Trade Groups. The traditional information-gathering tactic is active membership—or, more accurately, leadership—in professional groups, clubs, charities, and trade groups. Though people experience a wide range of effectiveness in these organizations, the usefulness of these activities in intelligence-gathering terms is proportional to the enthusiasm of the firm member. Everyone should engage in at least one activity outside of the business, if only for their own enjoyment.

Follow these guidelines for involvement in charitable, civic, educational, community, and cultural organizations:

○ Find something you enjoy doing, with results that are important to you. Don't join an activity or request a staffer to join an activity in which you have no interest, because it will always backfire.

○ Find out who belongs to or is involved with the group or activity. Ask your contact in the group to take you to some of the functions. If you are equally interested in several different activities, choose the one with the most information-gathering opportunities.

○ Ask your contact in the group how you can get involved and how you can help. Most organizations offer a variety of ways to assist, such as volunteering work, donating money, or donating your own skilled time. Contrary to popular belief, organizations are always looking for skilled volunteers. The people who run these organizations are usually business leaders, and results are their measuring stick. Your effort and results will build your reputation in their eyes, and will pay long-term information-gathering dividends. It is difficult to find a more positive image builder than to volunteer, work hard, and contribute something to an organization.

○ The importance of visibility cannot be stressed enough. The most visible spot within an organization is in the limelight of leadership. It can be difficult to attain, but larger institutions have many areas where you can help. They offer more choices, more flexibility, and generally more contacts.

○ Whatever you select, work at it. Make the time and work toward a position of importance (it is not enough to be a joiner). You will find that you learn a lot, meet interesting people, and improve your opportunities.

Conventions and Trade Shows. Showcasing your products and/or services in a booth at a trade show or convention is usually expensive, time-consuming, and rather unproductive. Nevertheless, if the industry or field is congruent with your customer base or a field you're attempting to enter, it could be an excellent source of intelligence. Check with your customers in the industry. Do they attend the convention? Will principals attend, or just salespersons?

166

What are their opinions of this trade show? Weigh this option carefully.

Chambers of Commerce.   Do you glance at your annual Chamber of Commerce dues and wonder what benefit you are receiving? You certainly aren't alone! But the local Chamber of Commerce is one of the most popular gathering places in any community. Many businesspersons and other professionals join just to take advantage of the extensive network of contacts this industry group provides. Like any other social function, Chamber of Commerce events complement the firm's other information-gathering strategies.

Social Functions.   Social functions and gatherings are ideal opportunities to meet and contact information sources. Without question, your firm should sponsor at least two social functions a year for customers and two for information sources. If you sponsor the function, you can arrange the makeup of information sources to your liking. The following guidelines are suggested:

- *Plan.* The single most difficult aspect of a social function is the planning. Select a date that coincides with a firm milestone. Promote the event as fully as possible; the more discussed an event, the higher the attendance. Involve as many of your personnel as possible—for goodness sake, remind them that they are ambassadors of the firm! They aren't there to talk to each other, but rather to talk with the invited guests.
- *Be unique.* You can ruin all your carefully laid plans if your function seems too mundane or contrived. As long as you're investing your time and money, why not invest some careful thought and planning?

    When one firm was asked to sponsor a hole in a local golf fund raiser, undoubtedly the tournament organizers thought it would do what most firms did, which was merely to place a sign at the firm's sponsored hole. But, with the blessings of the tournament organizers, this firm set up a soft drink and water bar with plenty of ice at the tee (it was the thirteenth hole, and the day was very hot). At the green, the firm gave away tournament survival kits, which included a golf ball, tee, golf hat, an insulated cup for keeping a beverage cool, and a golf towel, all imprinted with the firm's logo.

○ *Don't cut corners.* At the very least, the major costs of your function include appropriate food and drink for the season and function. Door prizes and giveaways are acceptable.

○ *Follow up.* If planning is the most difficult aspect of a function, the most important aspect of a successful social event is the followup. Encourage guests to leave their business cards, possibly as part of a door-prize drawing. Add the names from these cards to your firm's promotional mailing list. At least thank the attendees through a thank-you letter campaign.

The value of social functions lies in the followup. Merely hosting a social function will guarantee you nothing but the expenses of the function. After information sources, customers, and prospective customers have had the opportunity to see you, your managers, and your employees at a social function, there will be a residue of positive feeling among the people you wish to impress. You must develop relationships from that initial contact or the time, effort, and expense of the function will go to waste.

The owner of a rapidly growing company described his experiences: "Every year, without fail, I host an open house and a Christmas party, and I do it up big. I have nothing but the best hors d'oeuvres, the best bands playing, and I make sure all my people appear professional and mingle with our guests, not each other. Everyone feels at home, and they should. I make darn sure I contact all of the attendees after the event and see what happens from there." He estimated that he receives six times as much annual revenue as he spends in party expenses, as a direct result of those parties—not including the indirect, positive public relations resulting from the events. But more importantly, the intelligence he gathers in maintaining relationships justifies the expense.

○ *Separate your invitees.* If you can afford it, have separate functions for customers and for influencers.

○ *Mingle.* Be certain your employees mingle with the guests, not each other. This can be difficult for employees; they may not be accustomed to working with people. But there is no better time than the present, when everything is in their favor and they are on their own turf. Remember the following mingling hints:

- Ask attendees for their business cards. Add them to your contact list.
- Read their name tags. Don't forget their names; most people *do* forget names, and it is impressive (and memorable) when a businessperson remembers a contact's name.
- Know beforehand who will be there.
- Take time out to greet people who are entering unfamiliar situations.
- Remember that everyone is a potential contact or referral source.
- Cut short nonproductive conversations.
- Just before dinner (or other serious meals), approach and speak to the person you most want to meet. Then suggest sitting together to eat.
- If there is no target contact available, meet as many new people as possible.
- To move into a business conversation, ask social questions about a person's business (e.g., "How did you get into PCB manufacturing?").

169

- Don't be afraid to dispense advice. Many businesspersons are loath to spread their knowledge, but a small demonstration goes a long way. Think of it as offering free samples.
- Circulate.
- When talking with contacts, set appointments to meet in the future. Save the actual selling until later.
- Have fun. If nothing else, that is what you are there for.

Presentations to Information Sources

If you don't meet a potential referral source at one of the events listed here, you need to go straight to the referral source. Go to your largest customers and leverage off of their referral sources. Call them and ask for an appointment to introduce yourself and your firm. Ask them to bring a sidekick or two.

Prior to meeting with potential information sources, you need to establish a reason to meet. If you merely get together for lunch and exchange business cards and handshakes, you really haven't accomplished anything. Treat an influencer as if he were a prospective customer and bring something to the table. For example, there is a painting contractor who waits until a good customer needs a drywall contractor. When this occurs, he calls a drywall firm where he has had a few contacts. He asks to meet with one of the owners and lets the owner know that he has heard good things about them and their work. Would the owner have a few minutes to spare to sit down and discuss each other's companies and philosophies?

I adopted this same approach, and I have failed to meet with an influencer only 3 times in more than 230 approaches.

You might think that a prominent influencer would avoid you, especially if your firm is not very large. In actuality, a top influencer is anxious to meet all the good people she can. She is in that position because she is as good a salesperson as she is a technician, and being a good salesperson, she is accessible to anyone interested in a relationship.

The few influencers who have refused to meet with me were employed at large institutions. They eventually did meet with me and they let me know that not only would they not refer us any business, but also that they had never heard of our firm and that nothing I said would change their minds. They were rude, abrupt, and brusque. They refused to share any information at all.

One of these referral sources was a banker who didn't show up for our first meeting. He later said that he was able to get a starting time at the local golf course, and "you know how it is." That bank eventually faced record losses and was sold to one of the other statewide banks.

Obviously, not meeting with me didn't hasten the immolation of the bank, but I did find it indicative of the attitudes of unsuccessful people. It almost seemed as if they were trying to turn business away. These are not the kind of influencers who would be able to refer business to you in any event.

Meeting with Influencers

When you meet with an influencer, let him know how well you think of him and his company. Tell him how you learned of him, and launch into a conversation centered around *his* business and his needs. Find out what makes him tick.

When it is your turn to speak, identify and isolate the most positive aspects of your business. Choose the ones that should appeal most to him and his firm. Unlike the reasons a customer chooses a business, most other professionals have much narrower, self-serving views of what makes a terrific businessperson. They generally ask themselves the following questions regarding service firms:

- ○ *"Will she refer business to me?"* A primary concern for a fellow service provider is whether he can count on you to refer business to him. Assure him that, because you have heard excellent things about him and his firm, you will include them as one of your potential service resources. In fact, because you have several avenues for gathering new contacts, you can refer business to firms like his on a regular basis.

○ *"Will she produce her products or render her services on a timely basis?"* This is the second concern of people who refer you business. As long as your timeliness stays within agreed parameters, you will have no difficulties. If you provide him with the product or even a preliminary statement a week or more ahead of time, you will be well on your way to cementing the relationship.

○ *"Is her quality good enough?"* Every professional is cognizant of the varying levels of quality in professional industries, and they always worry about the quality of documents. If someone makes a decision based on your faulty numbers, your firm looks extremely bad. For this reason, many banks require financial statements from national accounting firms, out of hand, even for solid, well-established companies.

○ *"Is she easily accessible?"* Not being financial service persons, many fellow service providers want to know that a businessperson will be available to help interpret sections of the statements or lend advice. Of course, many service providers make themselves unavailable to bankers, preferring to spend their time being chargeable.

○ *"Will she share information?"* Information is the best free currency you have. Use it freely, use it wisely.

Presentations to Influencers Working with Current Customers

Call your customer's influencers. Chew the fat a bit. See how things are coming on your proposal, and ask if your work arrived on time (of course it did; you're on top of things, right?). This works in your favor with influencers.

Center your intelligence approach around what appeals to the influencer, and tell him again how impressed you are with him and his business. Your conversation need not be much different than with a prospective customer; in fact, your manner should be similar.

Before your presentation, the influencer probably expected an exchange of business cards and a vague promise to get together for lunch. But if the source impresses you enough to work with him, surprise him by inviting him to your office to speak with a prospective customer. He will be grateful for and impressed by this demonstration of your confidence in him.

SUCCESSFUL RELATIONS WITH INFORMATION SOURCES

Ten keys for a successful relationship with information sources are:

1. Introduce yourself.
2. Be enthusiastic about yourself and your firm.
3. Be curious about the source and his or her business.
4. Get involved with the sources in any way you can.
5. Exchange ideas on common problems.
6. Get to know emerging people (rising stars) rather than established people.
7. Don't ever avoid someone you have already met.
8. Use a tickler file database for information sources and potential customers. Make a point of touching base with every name on the list on a regular basis. (One manager has four dated tickler files for contacting his information sources on a weekly, monthly, bimonthly, and quarterly basis.)
9. Reciprocate all favors performed by contacts.
10. Get to know the local paper's business editors.

Remember to thank information sources. You need to guard referral source relationships with the methods and protection you give your own customers. When a referral source sends you a lead, make your appreciation clear. Sending thank-you letters to information sources should be routine.

CONCLUSION

In short, developing a solid referral base will accomplish seven major things that no business can do without:

1. It will provide you with a flow of customers.
2. It will provide you with positive references to prospective customers.
3. It will improve and promote your professional image and identity among the professional and business communities and the general public.
4. It will help modify your growth curve.
5. It will help attract quality, qualified staff.
6. It provides an impetus for growth.
7. It paves the way for negotiations with other professional services in your area.

8

Infoplan

Don't judge each day by the harvest
You reap but by the seeds you plant.
—Robert Louis Stevenson

WHY WE GATHER INFORMATION

Certain trends will always force the issue, including:

○ Increased competition within your industry
○ Increased competition from outside sources
○ Greater consumer and/or business selectivity

By gradually undertaking accepted information-gathering activities, we are able to actively promote and develop our businesses without relying on the vicissitudes and vagaries of the market.

Recall the definition of *information gathering*: the process of planning and executing the conception, pricing, distribution, and promotion of ideas, goods, and services to create exchanges that satisfy individual and organizational objectives. In short, information gathering is not a single activity; it is a synergistic process that utilizes a number of activities to achieve a set of goals.

There is no single way to develop information. One of the most frustrating things for a knowledge management professional to encounter are the many businesspersons who are certain that their way to build knowledge is the only way. Certainly you must be comfortable with the proposed information-gathering methods; however, it is imprudent to close one's mind to the wide range of options available. There are many ways to build a business, and different methods work better for different businesses.

In spite of the nature of business, people have different skills, goals, values, interests, market niches, and environments. The blend of these different combinations requires individual information-gathering plans for each business, with a variety of information-gathering activities. The object is to wring the maximum effectiveness out of the best possible combination of information-gathering activities for your business.

Just because some information-gathering methods seem foreign or different doesn't mean they won't work for you. Often the most effective methods for you are the ones you don't consider. Businesspersons ordinarily use tried-and-true methods simply because they have been used before. Just because people are comfortable with these techniques doesn't necessarily mean they will be successful, because businesses are unique.

There are no hard-and-fast rules for information-gathering success. In fact, practice development success often hinges on surprisingly mundane and isolated aspects of the business. We all know hard-working, competent businesspersons who seem to fight all their lives for market share, but remain at the subsistence level—and no one, least of all the professional himself, understands why he cannot grow. Essentially, these businesses have internal or environmental problems that hinder their growth ability. A program of information-gathering activities would reduce these obstacles, and could actually turn some obstacles into advantages.

WHY YOU MUST PLAN

Charging into information-gathering activities without first planning their use is a little like building an airplane without reading the instructions: You might make something that resembles what you want, but it will not fly. Haphazard use of information-gathering activities will create an unbalanced knowledge management program that yields mixed results at best.

No single information-gathering activity will produce the more desirable effects of a coordinated knowledge management program. In one instance, an extremely successful business coordinated all of its knowledge management activities. It gathered information both through telemarketing and research programs, which were complemented by a customer information-gathering program and supplemented through extensive networking. The business maintained an extensive central database of contacts and the managers discussed information gathering at each manager meeting. The firm employed a director devoted solely to gathering research, market data, and opinions, and the business updated all information-gathering programs, approaches, and plans on a regular basis.

A more insidious side effect of relying on only one or two information-aggregating methods is the false confidence that such limited information-gathering programs engender. Some businesses pour tens of thousands of dollars into market studies that study the competition from the outside, yet ignore critical word-of-mouth from key influencers.

A long-range, comprehensive information-gathering plan is vital for growth because it:

- Emphasizes the need to integrate diverse market inputs into a company's plans.
- Creates a psychological foundation among the business's management and employees for information gathering, knowledge management, and business development.

o Unites management and staff with an easily understood, common goal.

o Creates a balanced knowledge management program that improves the customer base and the business's reputation, and ultimately makes the business more profitable.

o Focuses effort on carrying out the plan.

Your information-gathering plan will fulfill your knowledge management objectives. Although you may have many stated objectives within the information-gathering program, they should boil down to just two: first, that you are there when a customer decides to change vendors or service providers; and second, that when a potential client decides to make a change, she thinks of your business.

In other words, you need to be in the right place at the right time. All other goals and objectives are subordinate to these two concerns.

THE PLANNING PROCESS

It is a shock when a company transforms itself from an organization that is passive towards information-gathering into one that effectively uses its knowledge base. A knowledge management retreat will prepare your organization for this all-encompassing change.

Plan a Knowledge Management Retreat

To promote satisfactory awareness among your management team and your employees, a knowledge management retreat is strongly recommended. A retreat is ideal for reducing distractions when taking any significant step that is both meaningful to and out of the ordinary for your business. Developing your knowledge management (KM) plan definitely fits in that category.

Try the following rules for planning a retreat:

○ *Take a few days.* Hold the information-gathering planning session over one or two days to emphasize the importance of the event and the project.

○ *Prepare and distribute the retreat agenda to all parties prior to the retreat.* Decide what you want to learn and where the information gaps are, and make certain that those items are part of the agenda.

○ *The setting should be secluded and businesslike, with few distractions.* Some businesses prefer a nonretreat setting and may convene instead at a manager's house for a day or two to escape the insistent pressures of the office.

○ *Participants should include all managers and anyone who will be involved in setting information-gathering guidelines or primarily responsible for implementing KM procedures.* Include anyone who will lead information-gathering activities. A person who is later assigned an information-gathering task but was not invited to the retreat could very well resent the task and resist the activity.

○ *One person must moderate the retreat.* If the business has engaged an experienced information-gathering consultant, he or she should facilitate the meeting.

○ *Do not allow any interruptions, except for emergencies.* Call in for messages twice a day (just before lunch and at afternoon breaks). Have all secretaries refer emergencies to the senior manager back at the office. He or she will be in charge of relaying the message to the managers.

Perform an External Information-Gathering Audit

Before your retreat, you will need as much market information on your business and industry as possible. This will entail making an accurate assessment of the market perceptions of your business. The audit is similar to a customer survey in that it gauges your business image vis-à-vis your referral source network. Because you are not seeking minute details, the audit is not as comprehensive as a customer survey; rather, it helps you more clearly perceive your market position. Further, it helps you to recognize the business community's perceptions of your business.

Most businesspersons have strong opinions of themselves and their firms. They rarely seek outside opinions on their performance, and when they do, it is usually from a few close friends. Consequently, most businesspersons harbor misconceptions of their reputations and images.

An external information-gathering audit is highly recommended. The audit involves informal interviewing of key people to construct a market image of your business. The list of interviewees should include existing customers, potential customers, information sources, bankers, attorneys, external industry experts, friendly competitors, and business journalists. Try to obtain their feelings on the following 14 topics:

1. To which firms do you like to refer business?
2. Which firms do you like best to which you *don't* refer business? Most people don't get this information, and this is the entire point of an information-development program: making yourself number two.
3. Which businesses are the rising stars?
4. Which businesses are the setting suns?
5. When you buy products or services or choose vendors, what influences your decision?
   - How much is influenced by quality?
   - How much is influenced by cost?
   - How much is influenced by communication?
   - How much is influenced by turnaround time?
   - How much is influenced by personal rapport?
6. What are the major limitations to growth in my profession or industry?

7. What are the major limitations to growth in contact industries?
8. Who are the key opinion leaders among information sources?
9. Where is the market headed?
10. What are the most important trends?
11. How does our business fit into the industry?
12. What are our strengths and weaknesses?
13. What do you like best about our business?
14. Where can we improve?

Certainly, you will not be able to touch on all these questions with all your sources, but try to get as much detail as possible.

An external information-gathering audit should not be considered a one-time-only activity; rather, it should be performed on an annual basis. Many businesses perform these audits semiannually, and some businesses even perform them on a rolling, quarterly basis with different participants. A few businesses perform them routinely with their existing and potential customers. Regular monitoring of your environment will detect changes in the firm's image and reputation more quickly and accurately than your position at the eye of the storm.

Though most businesspeople think they are in close contact with their customers and their marketplace, they rarely put their knowledge to the test of an information-gathering audit. Businesspersons often dislike the idea of an external information-gathering audit, but because the results are so important, I strongly urge all businesses to undergo such an audit prior to a knowledge management planning session.

Announce the Knowledge Management Plan to the Staff

Implementation of your information-gathering strategies will eventually involve your entire staff, so they should be notified when you develop the information-gathering plan. Everyone involved with the plan should expect to contribute to the eventual plan, and should have an idea of what to expect when the plan is put into effect.

It is tempting to bypass this step and dictate an information-gathering plan from the top. Try very hard to avoid this! An information-gathering strategy that is dictated to the business staff by one person is doomed to fail; all managers should buy into the Knowledge Management Plan (KMP). If your managers are not pulling in the same direction, they will work against each other.

Although you may not be able to have every employee at the retreat, seek qualitative information-gathering perceptions from your managers and department heads prior to the retreat. If this is your first formal brush with information gathering, it is possible that some or even most of your staff will be intimidated by the issues you discuss, if only because the issues are new. However, their input will help you to formulate the KMP.

Encourage the staff to brainstorm to uncover their abilities and true feelings about knowledge management, information-gathering activities, and the direction of the business. It is especially important to be solicitous when speaking with the staff. Focus on splits in the company, because people will be working on their own agendas. Divergences in business focus happen frequently among employees and staff at businesses that are oriented to information gathering, because "go-go" businesses tend to sweep little conflicts under the rug, and people may hide their true feelings. The problem is, those hidden feelings do exist, and could sabotage a business's information-gathering efforts.

Distribute Confidential Questionnaires

The individual in charge of gathering information should develop confidential information-gathering questionnaires for firmwide distribution. Prior to the retreat, the questionnaires should be completed and returned to the moderator, who then compiles the information and introduces the consensus.

Questionnaires (see later in this chapter for sample formats) should be completed by three separate groups:

1. *Senior management.* The retreat moderator must gauge the thoughts, positions, and feelings of the retreat participants *before* the retreat, so as to get an early impression of everyone's goals and desires.

   Many managers regard this questionnaire as unnecessary. Quite the contrary; it is one of the most important aspects of the planning process. It is notable that two people in a room will chat amiably; four people will express ideas they consider important; seven people will reduce input to intelligent conversation; in larger groups, people tend not to speak unless spoken to. In large-group situations, most people sublimate their personal feelings and thoughts to the conventional wisdom of the group. They believe that if their sympathies or ideas run counter to those of the group, they will lose standing and maybe respect. Consequently, as the group grows, total input declines.

   Information gathered from questionnaires can help overcome potential silences. This information will help facilitate candor during the meeting, and will serve as an excellent starting point for developing focus.

2. *Junior managers/junior partners.* The input of your future management is important. Compare their questionnaires with those of senior management. Are their responses significantly different from those of the managers? Why? Any significantly different response bears investigation.

3. *Staff and employees.* Although you may not reap anything of earth-shaking value, these questionnaires should be accepted in good faith, if only because your staff and employees have a different circle of contacts, and opinions and information may filter down to those individuals. At the very least, it's a different perspective on an existing intelligence base.

Compile and Organize Information

The retreat facilitator should compile the results of the external information-gathering audit, questionnaires, and research, and prepare an agenda for the meeting. The facilitator also needs to ensure that all details are taken care of, including the creation of any visual aids such as charts or graphs. Note paper and pens should be provided for each participant. The facilitator should be responsible for arranging refreshments. The facilitator's only role is to guide the meeting and keep it on track.

Conduct the Retreat

The retreat should begin at the same time as a typical business day. The meeting should include the following functions, in order.

Address by the Facilitator. The facilitator's address should:

- ○ *Greet the group.* Make everyone comfortable.
- ○ *Review the reasons for the information-gathering session.* This prevents the group from getting sidetracked and establishes a clear focus, goals, objectives, and an outline of information-gathering procedures.
- ○ *Review the agenda, ground rules, and procedures for the retreat.* State that participants must not be afraid to speak their minds; that brainstorming is a critical part of the process; and that any ideas or objections (at any time, for any reason) should be revealed immediately.
- ○ *Review the results of the external information gathering.* Exhibit the growth of the business during the previous year, the previous three years, and the previous five years. Use visual aids, such as growth charts. Review corporate growth, customer metrics, annualized revenue, cash flow, margins, and profitability. Review how much came from new customers, from expanded services to current customers, from rate

increases, from information sources, and from mergers and purchases. Do not include conjecture on the business's information-gathering image or reputation, but share opinions during the sessions.

○ *Review any previous information-gathering goals.* If goals were achieved, acknowledge this and compliment the group. Conversely, if goals were not achieved, state this as well. It is important that the group have a clear understanding of the firm's status before discussion begins.

○ *Review information-gathering questionnaires.* Begin with those completed by the senior managers. Give a thorough presentation of all comments, positions, and directions proposed by the managers. Next, review the results of the junior managers' information-gathering questionnaires, and finally, the staff and employee questionnaires.

Assess the Business's Current Position. Your reputation and image have been difficult to achieve; once lost, they are even harder to repair or regain. They are based on the history of your business and the local industry, your management strengths, the quality of your product, your ability and inclination to serve your customers, and even the personality of the managing manager.

Discuss your business's position with input from all managers. Take special care to respect everyone's views while reconciling serious deviations from the majority view. For instance, if a manager has stated that the business's image among a subset of customers is declining, but all other managers feel the business's image has improved, the comment should be explored.

Similarly, it defeats the purpose to react negatively to anyone's viewpoint when brainstorming; they will likely only become reticent about making further suggestions. The discussion should review all aspects of your current position, including:

○ *Your market and its growth potential.* How large is the potential market in your geographic area? How large can your business realistically grow? Is there a lot of business in the area, or is there already too little business spread among the competing firms? Describe your market. Is it mature? Do you need to develop new markets? By focusing on creating your market, as opposed to sharing a market, you begin with a huge advantage. When sharing a market, you are already somewhat handicapped by the existing competitors.

○ *Your business's image and reputation.* Review and discuss the results of your external information-gathering audit. What does the banking community think of your business? The legal community? Potential customers in target industries? How pervasive is your business reputation? How well have you spread a positive reputation?

○ *Quality of your services.* Have you had a peer review performed? What were the results? Solicit everyone's input, focusing first on external perceptions of your firm's work quality. Discuss the results of your peer review, if one was performed.

○ *Your headquarters.* How does your office contribute to your image? Is the exterior attractive? Is it accessible? Is parking convenient? Is your furniture attractive? How does your carpet look? What about the art? Are offices usually messy and disorganized, or neat and tidy?

○ *Your business's strengths and weaknesses.* Address strengths and weaknesses in their entirety. If employee or customer surveys have been distributed, these results should also be discussed. A particular weakness of many successful businesses is that they refuse to examine their weaknesses! Because some businesses are extremely successful, they can turn a blind eye to their own shortcomings.

After discussing the business's specific positions and capabilities, hold a roundtable discussion on the most important issues now facing the business.

Discuss Issues Affecting the Business's Information-Gathering Efforts.
This discussion should be aimed at managers as individuals and at
the business as a whole.

- *Quality.* Has your quality, or any aspect of your quality,
  adversely affected a contact's decision on whether to
  engage your business? Has it affected any referral source's
  opinion of your business? These are serious questions.
  Quite often, the business is the last to know whether its
  quality control is as diligent as it should be, and the business can suffer unknowingly.

    An IRS agent once said that each agent was expected to
  win a certain percentage of his or her audits. He mentioned
  that whenever he or one of his cohorts lost too many audits,
  they would request the file of a customer from a particular
  business. All the agents in the office were well aware of that
  business's marginal quality, and reviewed its customers' tax
  returns to improve their audit ratios. The firm itself was not
  aware of it.

- *Reputation and image.* You are constantly developing a corporate image. Describe it. Is it positive or negative? Does
  everyone fit into it? Your image is a reflection of all that
  occurs within your business. It affects the slant of opinion.

- *Service/product mix.* How does your product and service mix
  appeal to existing and potential customers? How does it
  stack up vis-à-vis the service mixes of your competitors? Are
  there any services or products that retreat participants
  would like the business to add or reengineer?

- *Timeliness.* How timely is your product? How timely are your
  responses to your customers? How fast do you return phone
  calls? What is timeliness adding to the perception of your
  quality?

- *Industry expertise.* How effectively are you using leads in
  target industries? How well do you know the movers and
  shakers?

○ *Communication.* How well are you communicating with your customers? Are you calling them, and taking the initiative in making contacts? How much information do they share with you? How much give and take is there? Do you have a systematic program of planning sessions with them? Do you socialize with them and contact them spontaneously? Do they use your research sources and seek your advice? Do they take your advice? Do they introduce you to their friends and their resources?

○ *Customer rapport.* How well does each staff member interact with the customers? Have there been any complaints? Are there any personality conflicts to be resolved? Do your staffers have rapport with customers? Are they developing market information? Do they secure enough—or *any*—knowledge?

○ *Information gathering.* How many contacts have you gathered during the past year? How many came from customers? From information sources? How many did your senior people get? Your junior people? How many did you get?

○ *Competitive advantages.* What are your competitive advantages and disadvantages in your target markets?

○ *Monitoring of information-gathering results.* How well do you monitor your information-gathering results? Are you aware of all areas that need improvement?

Discuss Knowledge Management Direction. A group agreement on the assessment of your information-gathering program provides a foundation for discussing the direction and positioning of your KMP in the future. After establishing the business's current position, you need to review the trends and dynamics of your market. Notice how they create the framework and frame of reference for defining your business's image and direction.

The direction of your information must be clear and acceptable to all. Often, both your internal and external information sources will attempt to wrest some information-gathering tasks from your internal knowledge management director. Do not allow this to happen! No graphic artist, designer, information-gathering director, or even information-gathering consultant can set your information-gathering direction for you, nor should they. Their input is valuable and should be considered, but the boss should make the final decisions.

Which direction should you take? The size of your business largely dictates the direction you will take in designing your KMP. Which category does your business fit?

- *Market leader.* If your business is a market leader, your goal is to maintain the practice and improve it where you can. The market leader has the highest percentage of quality customers in a market niche. These firms are respected, well known, and almost always considered when an established customer seeks proposals from businesses. Their referral source and information networks are extensive, and they command respect if only by virtue of their size and customer base. They have more access to more information sources than anyone else.

  Leaders usually block competitive moves by attacking smaller challengers. Smaller businesses typically avoid these attempted blocks by attacking the leaders' weaknesses: where they are least experienced, or where they are a fish out of water. For instance, a national business would compete with a regional business for its auto dealer customers, not its auto wash customers.

  Use market leader tactics to actively reach out to potential customers and information sources. These tactics should include frequent media appearances, public speaking, seminar presentation, and other public relations activities that confirm and consolidate your position as market leader. Make use of your strong referral networks and contact databases.

○ *First challenger.* The first challengers are the companies that rank directly behind the market leader in a market niche, yet are within striking distance of the leader. Their main consideration is the strength of the leading competitors in their market niche. These businesses will attack the leaders at the weaknesses that result from their strengths. For instance, a local business will attack a national business on its lack of personal attention for smaller customers. First-challenger businesses should realize that many companies in the same market niche will prefer the market leader for their work; small, privately held companies often seek out national businesses.

First challengers need to concentrate their attacks on a narrow front. They should not desire, nor could they service, many of the market leader's customers. They should remain content to hammer at the market leader's weakest niche. Information development activities should be limited, and first challengers should focus on developing their active networks (the half-dozen to three dozen companies that every businessperson should target as customers).

○ *Also-ran challenger.* Also-rans are smaller than both the leader and the first challengers. They do not have the resources, and aren't yet large or savvy enough, to challenge the market leaders. If they lure a customer away from a market leader, it is usually by accident or through a combination of unusual circumstances.

These smaller businesses have extremely limited resources and are at a disadvantage in the market. Expanding their service mix, partnerships, and mergers seem to be appropriate avenues for these businesses to develop information, along with strong development of their contact and network databases.

○ *Too small to challenge.* These businesses comprise the vast majority of small or sole proprietor businesses. They should find and hold a segment small enough to adequately defend. Businesses this small need to specialize in a particular industry, a very small geographic area, or in very small companies. These businesses should establish a unique service among their mix to appeal to customers in difficult marketplaces.

Their direction should not include many specific goals, but a general prediction of the future of the business. The discussion should include everyone's personal vision of the future and their places in this future. They should cultivate several information sources, of various types, to keep them abreast of their industries and what occurs within those industries.

Set Infogoals. After establishing your position and direction, you should soon reach a consensus of goals for:

o Competitor information
o Market information
o Opinion collection and filtering
o External research
o Internal analysis and dissemination

These guidelines should be created with your business philosophy and objectives in mind.

> If you don't know where you're going, every road will take you there.
>
> —Mao Tse Tung

Remember that proper definition of your business issues is key to successful information gathering. Proper definition of these issues and your market focuses your business's direction. By defining your market, you define your finishing point, and you can then create a target.

If you are the market or niche leader, you can charge higher prices, you have a broader reputation, and you can change your reputation faster than when you were an also-ran. Customers will be more loyal and you will attract better employees. You can penetrate the market faster and your service mix will gain greater credibility. Last but not least, you have more access to industry and other information sources.

Goal setting is an intricate practice, sometimes deceptively so. How does one estimate an individual's future performance, much less an entire business's performance, over the course of a year? It is difficult because there are so many factors to consider. Try the following blueprint for establishing goals:

- Set personal information goals before establishing business information goals. Business goals that are supported by individual goals succeed. Business goals that are unattached to individual goals fail.

- Each person sets his or her own goals. An excellent first step in establishing goals is to interview all participants candidly and allow them to establish their own goals. They, more than anyone else, are aware of their capabilities.

- Consider past performance. Realistic goals are developed in light of past performance. How much can someone realistically improve over the course of a year?

- Consider each employee's workload and future time schedule. Information-gathering results will correlate directly with the amount of time spent on information gathering.

- Consider each person's information-gathering capability. Staff and managers need to realize what they can and cannot accomplish.

- Set goals that create opportunities. Refrain from setting any finite goals. Goals should create opportunities and be open to revision during the year.

- Your goals should be measurable. Establish concrete goals as targets.

○ Set goals that preclude procrastination. Most people are born procrastinators. Create short- and long-term goals fit to each person. Each person and the moderator should set a time frame to complete the goal. Short-term goals help to focus employees and avoid procrastination.

○ Reward yourself and others after the attainment of goals. Be certain everyone is rewarded immediately after they accomplish their goals.

○ Consider your business's direction. Everyone's goals should support this direction.

Before you begin to generate business information, you should document and internalize definitive goals. Do you want to grow in a given industry? Do you want to develop a given service or product? Do you want to improve your professional reputation?

Be aware of all your information limitations, including:

○ Your industry contacts

○ Your current customer base

○ Lost customers and their impact on your market

○ Your professional networks

○ Your prospect base

○ External research and market data that you purchase

○ Information on your competitors and potential competitors

○ Prognostications, pro formas, future plans

○ Strengths and weaknesses of your management and employees

Set a timetable for achieving your information goals. After establishing individual goals, establish the business goals in each of the aforementioned areas. At the close of the retreat, write down all goals and have everyone sign the goal sheet. A copy of the goal sheet will be distributed to all managers and employees, and progress should be checked against the goal sheets on (at least) a quarterly basis. Assign a manager to check each participant's progress and report on the progress during a quarterly progress meeting.

After the business direction is discussed and goals are developed, you are ready to develop your information-gathering plan.

Develop the Information-Gathering Plan. Developing your plan essentially means applying your options to your goals. Your information-gathering plan will be the primary vehicle for:

○ Establishing your business's image, identity, and reputation
○ Creating a database of contacts
○ Disseminating information to the marketplace
○ Establishing and maintaining your network of information sources
○ Establishing ties to the media
○ Modifying your business's life cycle

There are several things to keep in mind when developing a information-gathering plan. First, remember that a small business is not a little big business. Small businesses are resource-poor, so they must minimize mistakes. This heightens the importance of a carefully considered information-gathering plan.

Secondly, mirror athletes who talk about "playing within themselves." They are referring to the practice of avoiding activities for which they are unsuited. The same holds true for information gathering. It is not necessary to copy another business's successful information-gathering techniques or service mix; in fact, it is undesirable. When choosing activities and methods, keep in mind the talents of your personnel.

Your plan will be based on the collective wants and needs of management. Your task is to reconcile everyone's varying desires and requirements so as to achieve the goals set forth in the previous section. The information-gathering plan should include the following aspects:

o *Mission statement.* Many management consultants advise entrepreneurs to articulate their purpose or mission in a single sentence or paragraph. If you can accomplish this, the idea is simple enough to be viable. If you cannot accomplish this, the idea is too complex to appeal to a common market.

Your information mission statement is similar to this statement of purpose, but has an added feature: It provides a single direction for everyone to follow. Many businesses use their mission statements almost as a mantra; they inculcate new hires with the mission statement from their first day with the business. The business's mission statement should illustrate the business's primary goals.

o *Time and resources devoted to information gathering.* How much time and money should the business spend on information gathering? Establishing a financial budget is relatively easy; many businesses merely take a small percentage of their gross revenue and allocate the funds to information gathering. There are disadvantages to this approach, because it emphasizes returns on the dollar and constricts the business's options—somewhat like telling a contractor you have a fixed amount of money to spend for a house before telling her what you want the house to look like.

It is more important to decide which information-gathering activities you will pursue, and how many employee and manager hours will be needed to accomplish them. Once you have decided this, you will be able to more appropriately apportion your investment.

o *Building the program.* One of the key reasons for maintaining an excellent information-gathering program is nurturing the business's future. Any business that establishes an information-gathering program must concentrate on the eventual outcome of the program.

o *Recruitment.* Your recruitment of both experienced and inexperienced accounting talent will significantly affect your information-gathering success. This area is overlooked to some extent at almost all businesses. Any experienced businessperson you hire will have, at the very least, an impact on your professional image and reputation. Your employees' technical expertise is the foundation of their success. Consider their information-gathering capabilities. Would you want them running your business in the future?

○ *Customer Turnover.* How much customer turnover is expected? If you manage out 15 to 25 percent of your customer base in one year, to accomplish the twin goals of pruning the deadwood and freeing additional time to market your services to a higher class of customers, you put yourself into position to derive more information.

All businesses lose some customers eventually, for varying reasons. Allow for a certain amount of turnover in the goals of your information-gathering plan.

○ *Mergers and acquisitions.* What are you looking for in an acquisition? Is it another geographic location? New expertise? Management help? Is it merely additional revenue? Whatever the reasons, you will most certainly develop more knowledge from the pursuit, by talking with the owners, their customers, their vendors, their contacts, their references, and so on.

The information-gathering director of a business that doubled in size every year for seven consecutive years claimed that her business did just two things to grow: first, the managers networked constantly; second, they considered every merger or acquisition candidate within a 30-mile radius. They maintained a state of readiness and were therefore not only open to the information they derived through negotiations of mergers and purchases, but they were also more adaptable to their market's dynamic environment.

Some businesses claim they will never consider a purchase or sale of another firm. However unlikely you consider this occurrence, you should at least plan for it by establishing the parameters within which you would consider a merger or an acquisition. That is sufficient for your interest.

○ *Information gathering in other locations.* It is an unfortunate fact of business life that the senior managers of companies tend to concentrate their information gathering in the home markets or the home offices. One six-office business experienced significant information development in the home office, but relegated the five outer offices to anecdotal information gathering. The home office had a very serious knowledge management program, but it left the other five offices to fend for themselves, which lowered morale among the outer offices.

Regional locations need care and attention, and your business's knowledge management efforts must both reach those outer offices and make use of the intelligence they gather. Frequently, they will have different insights; occasionally, they will have information earlier than the home office does.

○ *Customer retention.* Although knowledge management has many obvious benefits, it has some hidden ones as well. For instance, when developing a new information-gathering plan, many businesses expend most of their efforts on acquiring new business, while paying less attention to their current customers. It is very tempting to coast in established relationships, but you will find that most new customers have engaged your business for the quality communication they didn't receive from their former service provider. They necessarily will become excellent conduits of new information.

Unhappy customers create a mountain of headaches. Be certain that you have the time and energy for the information-gathering effort you are considering.

○ *Information gathering tactical mix.* Describe your information-gathering program. Is it the same one you used years ago? Do you need to devise new tactics? Do you require additional tactics in your information-gathering mix?

Target your tactics to a specific audience. Reevaluate the needs of your company, then create tactics to meet those needs. Before you employ a given information-gathering tactic, ask yourself the following questions:

- Is it a volume-driven tactic? In other words, will it create information flow on a regular basis?
- Does it fit into your current knowledge mix? Strangely, new tactics may obviate some old activities.
- Is it unique? If it is, that's not a bad idea. It should be a little bit different, or fill a slightly different information need than an already existing activity. A truly unique information-gathering tactic can produce rare knowledge.
- Who in your business wants the new information? What are its benefits? Will it contribute to your company's bottom line? How and why?
- Will they understand why they should want it? How will the information stand out? Can you sum up the knowledge derived in one sentence?

When devising your plan, be careful to choose methods and activities that are appropriate for the business. Use the following steps to decide on each information-gathering activity:

1. *Brainstorming.* Again, every manager and employee participates. Encourage participants to express all of their ideas, no matter how ridiculous or sublime, as long as there are sound information-gathering reasons behind them. Ask them their feelings on information gathering, information-gathering activities, the business's goals and directions, and their personal plans. Start with some general questions, like:

- Which direction is the business heading? Where will it be in five years? Ten years?
- Tell us about your personal direction. Where do you want to fit in with the business and its growth?
- What is your feeling about information gathering?
- What type of information-gathering activities would you be interested in?

Discuss both general and core intelligence needs, including:

- More referrals from current customers
- More referrals from information sources
- More cold leads
- Better intelligence on influencers
- Which businesses do influencers like best to whom they do *not* refer clients?
- Who are the rising stars in our industry?
- Are any competitors stagnating?
- When influencers buy or refer clients, what factors influence their decisions? How much is influenced by cost? How much is influenced by ease of delivery? How much is influenced by turnaround time? How much is influenced by personal rapport?
- What are the major limitations to growth in our industry?
- Who are the key opinion leaders among information sources?
- Where is the market headed? What are the most important trends?
- What is our market position?
- List our current services and products and their various uses for our customers. Include the appeal of each. Are we better than the competition? Worse? Why?

- List our customers' needs that we are not currently fulfilling. Please explain your answer.
- List the information we need to know about our current and future customers, competitors, and influencers.
- What kind of information goals do you feel our business should have?
- What do we need to do to reach these goals?
- How will you, personally, help the business arrive at that point? What are your personal information-gathering goals?
- What do you need to do and want to do to help improve the business's information-gathering performance?
- What information-gathering methods could the business use? What other methods could you make use of?
- How do you personally feel about information gathering? About sales?

2. *Discussion.* Review all the information-gathering alternatives with the employees. Have them do this little exercise as well—after all, they are the future managers. In the discussion, concentrate on the pros and cons of the information-gathering activities, the time involved, and the potential benefits of the activity.

3. *List all possible information-gathering alternatives.* You will find partial lists of sources in Appendix A and Appendix B.

4. *Grade the alternatives.* Using the checklist in Exhibit 8.1, have your employees rate their participation in the listed information-gathering activities on a scale from 1 to 10 (with 10 being the highest, and for a maximum total score of 100 points).

5. *Choose your information-gathering activities.* List the activities and the averages that each activity rated. You don't need to immediately implement those with the highest

Infoplan

Exhibit 8.1   Information-Gathering Activities Checklist

I diligently read industry periodicals and research the
    Internet for the purpose of generating applicable
    business knowledge   _____

I know and interact with senior influencers in my industry   _____

I know and interact with junior influencers in my industry   _____

I know and interact with people at our competitors   _____

I read research and analysis on our industry   _____

I contribute information, intelligence, and opinions to our
    collective knowledge base   _____

I freely interact with prospective clients and share opinions,
    information, and intelligence with them   _____

I freely interact with current clients and share opinions,
    information, and intelligence with them   _____

The information I generate influences the direction of our
    company   _____

I actively generate information on the strategies, people,
    and products of our competition   _____

Add the numbers for your employees and managers. This is the
information-gathering quotient (IGQ), which demonstrates their
information-gathering aptitude and desire and acts as an excellent
measurement of their information-gathering mentality.

---

numbers; instead, seek those activities to which the managers have assigned consistently high numbers. The activities you will want as part of your information-gathering
plan are those that have common appeal to the managers.

    Be careful when committing to specific information-
gathering activities. No matter what the size and niche of

your business, you need to follow a coherent information-gathering strategy. Keep these strategic information-gathering tips in mind:

- All aspects of your information-gathering activities should work together. Your information-gathering activities should be synergistic; used in concert, their effect is greater than the mere sum of individual efforts. Do not choose more activities than you can realistically control. You will get better results using fewer but well-chosen activities.

- Do not act like the market leader if you are not the leader. Market leaders use information and knowledge differently than other firms, both in the gathering and the administration of knowledge. A businessperson cannot declare himself the leader; the market (customers, potential customers, employees, and information sources) will perceive him as the leader when he really becomes it. Businesses that unduly act like the leader tend to lose market share through inaccurate focus.

- Do not act like a challenger if you are the market leader. When the leader acts like a challenger, it fails to employ all the information resources at its command. As the leader, it is unsuited to this position. A leader avoids confronting a challenger, unless it is to target the challenger's very best customers. A market leader does not have to worry about a challenger's mid- or lower-echelon customers.

- Hire away great competitors. If you can't beat 'em, join 'em. Some businesses prefer to compete by withdrawing from the marketplace. In one case, a small business grew tired of the intense competition in his area. The sole proprietor hired a manager from a national competitor, and within two years that former manager was bringing in millions of dollars' worth of customers to the business.

- Do not attack your competitors where they are strong. One consulting firm decided to open a separate litigation support department, even though a dozen other businesses already had existing litigation support departments. Though the business spent a great deal of time and money marketing to that niche, it all went for naught. The business stagnated and dropped the department after two years. A little bit of applied knowledge would have prevented that wasted effort.

- Using your knowledge management program, target your competitors' weaknesses. Even your strongest competitors have at least one weakness. For example, although a local business cannot hope to compete with a national business's expertise, it will always be less expensive, because of the different overhead burdens.

- Quickly apply your knowledge to decrease your turn-around time. Do not give your competition time to match you. When you use a particular information-gathering approach or decide to market a different product or service, hit the market fast. When delivering your everyday compliance products, seek ways to return the product to the customer faster.

- Do not be afraid to copy intelligence-gathering approaches, but do it quickly. This allows you to strengthen your market and weaken your competitor's market push.

- When implementing your plan, convince your people that they are the best—but don't *you* believe it. They aren't necessarily superior to your competitors' employees, but for motivational purposes, it's a good idea for them to believe it. Convey to them that your business is wonderful in large part because they are your employees.

Most competition is won through superior numbers. Although you may not have a superior number of people compared to your competition, you can and should have a superior number of knowledge management professionals. Train and motivate your staff and managers to actively seek information on the competitors, markets, clients, and so on, and you will have a potent knowledge management force.

- Dissemination is half the key to a successful information-gathering program. Every player wants to score touchdowns, but every coach will tell you that defense wins ball games. For businesspersons, *defense* equates with internal dissemination of existing (or easily accessed) information. When disseminating to your employees, take care that they have the appropriate analysis of (or are capable of analyzing) the information. It should be used to positively affect the service, communication, and timeliness you give your current customers.

- Do not make predictions based on faulty information. The first prediction that fails to come true will undermine your knowledge management program, to say nothing of your credibility. Instead, speak of goals that you all work toward and information categories. This will instill the same motivation and pride in your staff, as well as inspiring attention to the marketplace.

- Study your competitors' positions. Gather as much market information on your competitors as possible. This is especially important because this form of information can be very difficult to compile.

- Keep market trends and dynamics in mind while positioning your business. It is folly to build a information-gathering plan around outdated products and services. In fact, most businesses would agree that it is the height of idiocy to back a service or product that makes an business obsolete.

- The main consideration for a new product is the strength of the opposition's product. If your competition has a strong service or product with which you would like to compete, it is better that you pour your resources into developing information on it. Competing against entrenched opposition can be an information-gathering black hole; money and resources go in, but no customers come out.

- Focus your resources behind your best tactics and be prepared to abandon poor or incorrect knowledge. Push the lion's share of your resources into successful information-gathering methods, and cut your losses by ceasing information-gathering activities that don't work out.

- Develop positioning allies. Whatever information-gathering techniques you choose, it is important to develop aids that help position your business (e.g., referral networks, training coalitions, etc.) in a positive light.

- Don't use information-gathering methods that you have no business using. Is yours a small company? Does it need to spend $10,000 for the most up-to-date research, or can it get by with $2,000 for 6-month-old research?

- Focus on intangible intelligence factors; that is, factors and metrics that aren't immediately apparent to the competition. One analyst reviews more than 800 variables for a given industry. How many do you examine?

- Make sure your information-gathering activities fit into your corporate culture. For example, in some businesses, oddly enough, it is virtually taboo to interview former customers, even though that is one of the most fruitful means of analyzing dissatisfaction.

6. *Critique your plan.* Criticize and change it. Have all managers review the list of information-gathering activities and offer their input, both positive and negative. Include the employees' list of preferred information-gathering methods and review their input to get an idea of management's comfort level.

7. *Ask for volunteers.* Ideally, each activity should be implemented by the manager who originated the idea. However, as this isn't always possible, the next best action is to seek volunteers. Volunteers usually put more energy into an activity than appointees.

8. *Put your plan in writing.* Format the information-gathering activities and add them to the goal sheet. Each manager should sign the goal and information-gathering activity sheet, thereby formalizing his or her commitment to the program's success.

   - Turn it into a "planning for knowledge" calendar. Put the tasks and dates of completion on the calendar.

   - Perform information audits. Double-check the quality of the information you receive. Have a plan to do so.

   - Install fail-safes to solve intelligence shortfalls. After you have developed your key knowledge metrics (e.g., Who are the most vulnerable competitors? Which clients are closest to making a change? Which influencers like us and which don't?), plan on having at least two, and preferably three, different methods of gathering similar information.

   - Design superior contact management. One of the most neglected areas of information gathering is the cold prospecting that your company does.

9. *Review the plan.* There are a number of things you must attend to now that you have completed your information-gathering plan:

- *Investment.* Realize that the program is an investment, not an expenditure. It is doubtful that you will see immediate results. There is no way to tell if the plan is working during the first two months. Indeed, your patience directly affects your profits.

  Give your information-gathering plan a minimum of a month (better yet, three months) before you expect significant intelligence. When I started my first information-gathering plan, I did not have a solid, meaningful profile on a single competitor, despite spending 50 hours per week information gathering. But by the end of the year, I knew each one of my competitors inside and out.

- *Commitment.* You must be committed to the information-gathering plan. If you are not committed, your program will fail.

- *Consistency.* People must train successors for information-gathering tasks. Your program must be consistent; don't change horses midstream. Don't change your gathering methods, or your analysis. Don't drop sources and do not change your tactics! Train successors for their information-gathering responsibilities, to ensure consistency and program commitment.

- *Followup.* Have monthly meetings with all people who are heading an information-gathering activity to discuss progress, to restate or reestablish goals, and to rework old ideas and add new ones.

- *Customers.* Be certain that you do not neglect your current customers. They exist in the same markets you do, and should be your best source of new intelligence.

I am frequently asked, "What is the secret to gathering intelligence from customers?" Most people feel that their customers should realize that they want applicable intelligence. The secret is simple: Put yourself in your customer's shoes and ask yourself "What's in it for me?" When you have figured it out, ask the customer for the business.

After the Retreat

Undoubtedly, everyone back at the business will be quite curious as to what was accomplished at the information-gathering retreat. Immediately after your return, do four things:

1. Distribute the information-gathering plan to all major implementers, including the managers.

2. Distribute the goal sheet to all employees. This will outline the business direction to the staff.

3. Call a departmental or firmwide meeting to discuss the results of the retreat. During the meeting(s), request volunteers for the information-gathering activities. Every volunteer should sign the information-gathering plan under his or her individual activity. The purposes of these meetings are twofold: first, to select likely participants for information-gathering activities; and second, to focus the business's efforts on the information-gathering plan.

4. Do not announce your information-gathering plan to your customers, but ensure that you get their support. Make sure they perceive the benefit to them: better timeliness, better communication, higher quality, broader services, whatever.

WHY INFORMATION-GATHERING PLANS FAIL

The best laid schemes o' mice an' men [often go awry].
—Robert Burns

A well-prepared, well-executed information-gathering plan will be an enormous success. By following the instructions throughout this book, you should enjoy significant practice development success with your business.

Information-gathering plans fail for many different reasons. You will have considered all your business's strengths and weaknesses, service mix, competition, and your ideal information-gathering avenues; still, problems exist that can undermine an otherwise strong information-gathering plan. These problems include:

- *Sources.* Successful intelligence collection must take into account several psychological factors. As a rule, people tend to share information for irrational reasons. You have probably already learned that just because it is practical and sensible for someone to give up market information, it doesn't always ensure that they will do so on a regular basis.

  As you collect intelligence, you must be especially wary of the impact that your collection methods have on the sources. If you treat them fairly and honestly, they should be excellent, long-term sources. If they share information that comes back to haunt them, you will not only lose the source, you will lose its support as well.

- *Your employees.* In spite of the noise employees make about wanting change, most employees would like to be assured that their jobs will be relatively the same five years down the road. It is natural for employees to desire to maintain their common, routine activities. An intelligence-gathering plan dictates that your company will change, that the knowledge inputs will most definitely change—and that threatens employees.

  Even the smallest of businesses have created a semblance of gathering information, a method and manner of intelligence gathering. It is axiomatic: the larger the business, the more entrenched the methods. Internal compliance with your new information-gathering plan will depend on these factors:

- The degree to which your information-gathering plan and activities affect your established intelligence-collecting methods.

- The degree of open-mindedness to change among your employees.

- The degree of emphasis you place on your information-gathering plan.

○ *Your business's acceptance of change.* Businesses live and die according to how well they accept and thrive on change in their marketplace. If your competitors (both within and without your industry) encourage change within the industry, you must find out, and you find out through your intelligence-gathering program.

○ *Your managers.* Are all of your managers behind your information-gathering push? Undoubtedly, a percentage of them will resist the information-gathering effort to a variety of degrees, in a variety of ways, for a variety of reasons. This is why it is so important to make certain everyone is pulling in the same direction; otherwise, one or more employees may sabotage your information-gathering efforts (inadvertently, of course).

○ *"Perfect information market" mentality.* If you take the attitude that the information you gather is the same as that of your competitors—or worse, that the market reflects all available information—you have undermined your information-gathering program at its foundation. Your products and services are differentiable from those of your competition, and so are your information-gathering plans.

○ *Unforeseen circumstances.* Legislation, the introduction of new competitors (or products or services), a severe recession or industry slump, a horde of new businesses springing up, poor health or retirement of managers or key employees, and dry information markets are all examples of circumstances that can adversely affect your intelligence-gathering efforts.

○ *You.* Information gathering should come naturally to you, but the talent still must be nurtured. As the developer and main implementer of the information-gathering plan, you are the foundation of your business's information-gathering policies. You must have the creative thinking to conceive the plan, the courage to implement it, the stamina to review it, and the open-mindedness to alter it when necessary. Fear, uncertainty, and doubt are your enemies.

○ *Ignorance of the competition.* If you ignore the competition when you develop and implement an information-gathering plan, you are depending on luck for the success of the plan. Competitors are not stagnant. They do not sit still. They have their own means of gathering intelligence.

Any combination of these obstacles will hinder or stall your plan. Examine the possibility of these occurrences when developing your information-gathering plan and formulate ways to combat them.

CONCLUSION

Ideally, your information-gathering plan should be your road map for information-gathering success. To recap, let us review the keys to a successful information-gathering plan:

○ Use the input from everyone who will participate in the information-gathering plan, to achieve the best focus.

○ Write the plan yourself. There is no single successful method for information gathering, so keep your information-gathering strengths in mind when designing your program.

○ Make your plan integrated. Any business that uses just one or a few information-gathering activities will have a lopsided plan with uneven success at best. At worst, an uneven plan permits the vagaries of the market to define your business and shape your contact flow.

○ Target your natural contacts and information sources. Just as you should undertake your best information-gathering activities, 80 percent of your information-gathering effort should be directed toward your current contacts and information sources.

○ Monitor and evaluate your progress through an information-gathering audit.

○ Check your inner balance. It is no coincidence that the best information gatherers tend to be insecure rather than complacent. Beware complacency; it breeds poor quality. Balance, organization, and aggressiveness are the keys to successful knowledge management.

Conclusion

THE FUTURE OF KNOWLEDGE MANAGEMENT

As businesses evolve more and more sophisticated means of gathering, aggregating, and evaluating intelligence and information; and as they learn to disseminate and act on knowledge, the competitive nature of the market will continue to increase in intensity. Given that it has become increasingly difficult to achieve significant advantages through labor, overhead, materials, or other costs, it has become imperative for organizations to rely on the judicious use of information developed outside of their organizations.

THE LAST COMPETITIVE ADVANTAGE

Information cannot exist in a vacuum, however. It has no value unless it is analyzed, evaluated, and judged for usability, then applied in the appropriate manner. In this way you will achieve a significant advantage over your competitors. Your ability to accumulate and organize your business intelligence, and to ensure that employees have adequate access to it, will determine your ultimate advantage over your competition.

WHERE TO FIND ADDITIONAL INFORMATION

Information of all grades can be found at a variety of sources, including:

- Research and analysis firms
- Data and information firms
- Investment banks
- Consulting firms
- Independent analysts and researchers
- Professional service firms and large corporations
- Research universities
- Pay web sites
- Secondary resources
- Think tanks
- The free Internet
- Research institutes
- Trade organizations and industry associations

A partial listing of these sources are found in Appendix A and B.

Appendix A

Information Associations

This is a very brief list of associations devoted to information, intelligence, and knowledge management. It is by no means an exhaustive summary, but provides you with some resources to pursue additional intelligence and expand your knowledge management capabilities.

American Information Gathering Association
http://www.information gatheringpower.com/

American Management Association (AMA)
American Management Association International is the world's largest membership-based training organization.
http://www.amanet.org/index.htm

American Productivity & Quality Center
The American Productivity & Quality Center (APQC) is the resource for process and performance improvement for organizations of all sizes and industries. Through benchmarking, it can help you identify and adapt best practices to improve your productivity.
http://www.apqc.org/

Appendix A   Information Associations

**American Society for Information Science and
Technology (ASIST)**
Provides education and networking opportunities to information
professionals (including librarians, webmasters, information specialists, educators, researchers, publishers, information center
managers) in organizations around the world. Bridges the gap
between information science research and information services
practice.
http://www.asis.org/

Association for Information Management (Aslib)
Aslib actively promotes best practice in the management of information resources, and represents its members and lobbies on all
aspects of the management of and legislation concerning information at local, national, and international levels.
http://www.aslib.co.uk/

**The Knowledge Management Benchmarking
Association (KMBA)**
KMBA conducts benchmarking studies to identify practices that
improve the effectiveness of knowledge management activities.
http://kmba.org/

Knowledge Management Consortium International
Knowledge Management Consortium International aims at
organizations and individuals coming together to develop a
shared vision, common understanding, and aligned action about
knowledge and knowledge management.
http://www.kmci.org/

Appendix B

Sources of Information and Analyses

This is a lengthy list of organizations engaged in providing information, intelligence, knowledge, research, analysis, and opinions on a variety of industries and topics. It also includes some interesting links that are useful for information-related purposes. Again, the list is not exhaustive. All contact and URL information is accurate as of this writing.

Source Name	Location	Type
100hot	www.100hot.com	Best web pages
About.com	www.about.com	Q&A
Acronym Finder—Hi Tech	www.mtnds.com	Directory
ADSL Forum Public Area	www.adsl.com/adsl_forum.html	Industry-telecom
Alexa	www.alexa.com	Search tools
All Business.com	www.allbusiness.com	Business research
Alta Vista	www.altavista.com	Search tools
ALTS-Association for Local Telecom Services	www.alts.org/	Industry-telecom
American Society of Association Executives	www.asaenet.org/Gateway/onlineAssocSlist.html	Associations
American Committee for Interoperative Systems	www.acis.com	Associations
AMR Research	www.amrresearch.com/	Company information
Annual Report Service	www.annualreportservice.com	International-(UK) annual
Annual "Reports UK" Reports	www.carol.co.uk/reports/index.html	Anonymous Web Access
Anonymizer	www.anonymizer.com/net	International-(UK) companies
AppleGate Directories (UK)	www.applegate.com	Metasearch engines
Ask Jeeves	www.askjeeves.com	Associations
Association for Computing Machinery	www.acm.org	Technology reference
ATM Forum	www.atmforum.com	Customer satisfaction
Better Business Bureau	www.bbb.org	Stock quotes
Bloomberg	www.Bloomberg.com	Business links
brint	www.brint.com	

Name	URL	Category
British Telecom Yellow Pages	www.eyp.co.uk/	International-(UK) phone book
Broadband Guide News	www.broadband-guide.com/news.html	Industry-telecom
Broadcasting & Cable Yrbk	Nexis-BRDCBL in BUSREF, CMPGN, LEGIS	Directory
Business Communications Co.	Dialog- /	Market research reports
Business Journals	www.amcity.com	Media
Business Wire	www.businesswire.com	Technology reference
business2	www.business2.com	News & magazines
C4-Parallel Search Technology	www.c4.com/	Search tool
Cable on Demand News—Media	www.catv.org/GIP/news	Industry-telecom
California Wireless-Wireless Links	wireless.com/interesting.html	Industry-telecom
Cellular Phone Info (consumer)	www.point.com	Industry-telecom
Center for Business Research/PW Post	www.liunet.edu/cwis/csp/library/cbr/cbrvl.htm	Library-business
CEOexpress	www.CEOexpress.com	Business links
Chatscan	www.chatscan.com	Search tools
cif1	www.cif1.com	Market research
cmpnet	www.cmpnet.com	News & magazines
CNET.com	home.cnet.com	Business links
CNNfn-financial network	cnnfn.com/	News & magazines
companiesonline	www.companiesonline.com	Company information
Company Annual Reports Online (CAROL)	www.carol.co.uk	Company information
Company House (UK)	www.companies-house.gov.uk/frame.cgi?OPT=free	International-(UK) companies
companysleuth	www.companysleuth.com	Company information
Computer Economics	www.computereconomics.com	Research site
Computer Technology Industry Association	www.comptia.com	Associations

(continues)

219

Source Name	Location	Type
Computerized Facility Integration	www.bestpractices.com	Outsourcing
ComputerWire	www.computerwire.com/	Industry Information
Computing Directionary	wombat.com.ic.ac.uk/foldoc/index.html	Directory
Copernic Plus	hotfiles.zdnet.com/cgi-bin/texis/swlib/hotfiles/info.html?fcode=000PB	Search tools
Corporate Information	www.corporateinformation.com	Research aggregator
Corporate Reports (UK-Annual Reports)	www.corpreports.co.uk/index.html	International annual reports
Cyberskeptic Guide	www.bibliodata.com	Web-update
Dailystocks	www.dailystocks.com	Stock quotes
Datamonitor	Dialog- /	Market research reports
Dataquest	www.dataquest.com	Market research
Debriefing	www.debriefing.com	Meta search engine
Deep Canyon	www.deepcanyon.com	Research aggregator
DejaNews	www.dejanews.com	Discussion
Demand Research (executive find)	www.demandresearch.com	People
Dialog Webtop	www.webtop.com	Business information search
Dictionary Resources	www.med.usf.edu/~yyao/dictionary.html	Reference
Digital Subscriber Line Forum	www.adsl.com	Associations
Directory of US Exporters	CD-ROM	Nexis/Dialog
Discount Long Distance Digest	www.thedigest.com/	Industry-telecom
Ditto	www.ditto.com	Search tools
djinteractive	www.djinteractive.com	General news
DJI-Publication Library Sources	ask.djinteractive.com/content/PubDir/pubdir.asp	Publications directory
Dogpile	www.dogpile.com	Search tools

Name	URL	Category
Doing Business Research on the Web	www.pitt.edu/~refquest/business/	Business research
dot.com Directory	www.dot.com	Company information
Dow Jones Business Web Directory	www.businessdirectory.dowjones.com/	Directory
DSL-Digital Subscriber Line	www.dslcon.com/	Industry-telecom
E*Journal	www.ecarm.org/journal	Journal-E-commerce
ecommercetimes	www.ecommercetimes.com	News & magazines
EIU Market Research	Dialog-	Market research reports
Ejemoni	www.ejemoni.com	Search tools
Ejournals	www.library.ubc.ca/ejour/	Ejournals
Electronic Business Management Magazine	www.eb-mag.com/	Ejournal
Electronic Commerce News, Sources	www.allec.com/	News
Electronic Commerce World	www.ecomworld.com/	Business Link
Electronic Industries Alliance	www.eia.org	Associations
Electronic News	www.pcgv.com/news.html	News
eLibrary	[www.elibrary.com]	Web search
Email mailing lists	www.copywriter.com	E-mail addresses
emarketer	www.emarketer.com	Market research
Enterprise Storage	www.infostor.com	Data storage
Entrepreneur World	www.entreworld.com	Entrepreneur resources
Escribe	www.escribe.com/library/business/	Reference
ESPICOM Telecom/Power Rpts	Dialog-	Market research reports
Euromonitor Mkt Research	Dialog-	Market research reports
European Companies	www.eurpages.com	International -Company
European Government Research	www.gksoft.com/govt/en/europa.html	International

(continues)

Source Name	Location	Type
Everything E Mail	www.everythingemail.net	E-mail addresses
Excite	www.excite.com	Search tools
EXP.com	www.exp.com	Q&A
Expert Central	www.expertcentral.com	Consumer expert site
Export Hotline (UK)	207.121.156.3/isiweb/toc/asp/w2tocmc.asp?TOCCODE=72	International Market Research
fastcompany	www.fastcompany.com	News & magazines
Faulkner Information Services	www.faulkner.com/	Research
FCC-State Link	www.fcc.gov/ccb/stats	Industry-Telecom
fedstats.gov	www.fedstats.gov	Government/statistics
Financial Review Dictionary	www.country.com/au/dict.htm	Financial information
Financial Services Professional Online	www.fsonline.com	Financial information
Find/SVP	Dialog- /	Market research reports
FINDEX	Dialog-	Market research reports
Forrester Research	www.forrester.com	Market research
Free Pint	www.freepint.co.uk	Web-update
The Freedonia Group, Inc.	Dialog- /	Market research reports
FreeEdgar Reference Tools	www.freeedgar.com/reference/tools/	Reference
Frost & Sullivan	Dialog- /	Market research reports
FSC-Net Directory	fsc.fsonline.com/netdir.html	Industry-Telecom
Fuji-Keizai Mkt Research	Dialog	Market research reports
Fuld & Company	www.fuld.com	Research
Gale Directory of Publications	www.galenet.gale.com	Publications directory
Gale Encyclopedia of Associations	Dialog- /	Associations

Garage.com	www.garage.com	Startups
GartnerGroup Interactive	gartner12.gartnerweb.com/public/static/home/home.html	IT Industry Research
Giga Information Group	www.gigaweb.com	IT Industry Research
Global Internet 100 Survey98	www.info-strategy.com/GI100/	Internet surveys
globalfindata	www.globalfindata.com/links.htm	Company information
go2net	www.go2net.com	Metasearch engines
Google	www.google.com	Other search engines
Government Information Locator Service	www.access.gpo.gov/su_docs/gils/browse-gils.html	Government links
Harvard	www.hbsworkingknowledge.hbs.edu	Business Portal
Harvard Business School library	www.library.hbs.edu/	Library
hbsp	www.hbsp.com	Business cases
Head-to-head (Online)	www.onlineinc.com	Web-update
HM Customs & Excise Information Svc	www.hmce.gov.uk/	International-(UK)
Homework Helper	www.education.elibrary.com	Education links
Hoover Industry Snapshots	www.hoovers.com/features/industry/industries.html	Industry
Hoover's Inc	www.hoover.com	Company
HotBot	www.hotbot.com	Search tools
Hotwired	www.hotwired.lycos.com	Media
IAC Business & Industry	Dialog-	Industry
IAC PROMPT	Dialog-	Industry
IACTrade & Industry	Dialog-	Industry
idc	www.idc.com	Market research
IEEE	www.ieee.org	Industry information

(continues)

Source Name	Location	Type
IEEE Computer Society	www.computer.org	Computers
iMarket Inc.	www.imarketinc.com/	All
Industry Insider	www.investex.com/Investex/index2_RBWlink.html	Associations
The Industry Standard	www.thestandard.com	News & magazines
inference	www.inference.com	Metasearch engines
InferenceFind	www.infind.com/	Directory
Information Resources Links	www.ais.org.ge/links.html	Links
Information Society Initiative 4 Business	www.isi.gov.uk/	International-(UK) Industry
Information Technology Assn of Amer	www.itaa.org	IT
Information Today, Inc.	www.infotoday	Links
Information Week	www.informationweek.com	Research
Infozech Telecom Information Resources	www.infozech.com/resources.html	Industry-Telecom
Integra	www.integrainfo.com	Financial (PRV)
Intel/Microsoft	www.trivergence.com	Alliances
International Telecommunications Union	www.itu.int/	Telecom
Internet Public Library	www.ipl.org/re/aon	Business links
Internet Search Advantage	www.cobb.com/isa	Web-update
Internet Sleuth	www.isleuth.com	Search tools
Internet World E-Business & Internet Technology	www.internetworld.com/	Internet Industry

Name	URL	Category
InternetNews Magazine	www.internetnews.com	News & magazines
Invest in France Agency (IFA)	www.investinfrancena.org	International-(France) market/industry
Investment Research	www.investex.com/Dialog-/Nexis-	Market research reports
IPO Express	www.edgar-online.com/ipoexpress/	IPOs
IPV6	www.ipv6.com	Internet protocols
ISDN Org	www.isdn.org	Telecom
ISP-C Internet Srvs Providers' Consort	www.ispc.org	Industry-Telecom
ISP-CLEC Online Magazine	isp-lists.isp-planet.com/isp-clec/	Industry-Telecom
Ithaca Company Net	www.ithaca.edu/library/biblio/companynet.htm	Search tools
Ithaca Library	www.ithaca.edu/library/biblio/comp798.htm	Search tools
iWon	www.iwon.com	Other search engines
Javelink	www.javelink.com/cat2main.htm	Alert-web
JUGHEAD's DataComm Library	teleport.com/~jughead/modem_library.htm	Industry-Telecom
Jupiter Market Research	Dialog	Market research reports
Just in Time Article Delivery	www.public.iastate.edu/~CYBERSTACKS/just.htm	Clippings service
Librarians' Index to the Internet	sunsite.berkeley.edu/InternetIndex/	Directory
Librarians' Resource Center	www.sla.org/chapter/ctor/toolbox/resource/index.html	Directory
Listserv of Listserv	juliet.stfx.ca/people/fac/rmackinn/listserv.htm	Listserv
Liszt	www.liszt.com	Search tools
Market Guide Inc-Financial Information	pcn.marketguide.com/MGI/	Financial information
marketguide	www.marketguide.com	Company information
MarketLine Int'l (snaphots Intl)	Dialog-/	Market Research reports
MarkIntel (Research Bank Web)	www.investex.com	Market Research reports

(continues)

225

Source Name	Location	Type
mckinseyquarterly	www.mckinseyquarterly.com	Business cases/publications
MediaFinder	www.mediafinder.com	News
Mergerstat (M&As)	www.mergerstat.com/index.html	Mergers & acquisitions
MetaCrawler	www.metacrawler.com	Search tool-Meta
Michigan State Univ CIBER	ciberbus.msu.edu/busres.htm	Library-business
Moneynet	www.Moneynet.com	Stock quotes
Motley Fool	www.fool.com/	Financial Information
Multex	www.multex.com	Financial
myresearch	www.myresearch.com	Analyst reports
NASD, Inc	www.nasd.com/	Public Company Info
National Institute of Standards & Technology	www.nist.gov/welcome.html	Standards Research
National Technical Information Services	www.usgovsearch.com/Dialog-6	Research-Engineer
NCC-ISP & Telecom Info	www.com-broker.com/servlist.htm	Industry-Telecom
NetGuide	www.netguide.com	Internet Research
netlingo	www.netlingo.com	Technology reference
Network Solutions Inc. (NSI)	www.networksolutions.com	Web-Domains
Network World	www.nwfusion.com	network
news	www.news.com	News & magazines
News Resources	www.value.net/downtown/newsrsrc.html	News
Newspapers Database	www.newspaperlinks.com/framesFiles/framesContent.asp	News
NewsTrawler	www.newstrawler.com	Media
Northern Light	www.nlsearch.com	Search tool

226

Northern Light	www.northernlight.com	Search tool
Notess	www.notess.com	Search tools
nua.ie/surveys/index.cgi	www.nua.ie/surveys/index.cgi	Surveys
odci.gov/cia/publications/factbook	www.odci.gov/cia/publications/factbook	Government/statistics
Office.com	www.office.com	Business research
Official Catalog of Listservs	www.lsoft.com/lists/listsref.html	Listserv
Oingo	www.oingo.com	Search tools
OneSource	www.onesource.com	Market research reports
Online Computing Dictionaries	www.nyise.org/dictionary.htm	Directory
Online Investor (OLI)	www.investhelp.com	Mergers & acquisitions
Online Strategies	www.onstrat.com	Search tools
Open IPO	www.openipo.com	Financial
PC World Online	www.pcworld.com/	Periodical
Planet IT—For IT Professionals	www.planetit.com/	IT Industry
PointCast	www.pointcast.com	Search engine
Power Search	www.deja.com/home_ps.shtml	Search engine
Powerize	www.powerize.com	Infromation agreggator
Practice Database	www.practicedatabase.com	Best practices
Price—Congressional Research Service	gwis2.circ.gwu.edu/~gprice/crs.htm	Search tools—Government
Price—Direct Search	gwis.circ.gwu.edu/~gprice/direct.htm	Web-Links
Price—Direct Search (bibliography)	gwis2.circ.gwu.edu/~gprice/bibs.htm	Search tools—Bibliography
Price—Direct Search (cities)	gwis2.circ.gwu.edu/~gprice/state.htm	Search tools—Databases
Price—News Center	gwis2.circ.gwu.edu/~price/newscenter.htm	Web-Links

(continues)

Source Name	Location	Type
Price—Speech & Transcript Center	gwis2.circ.gwu.edu/~gprice/speech.thm	Search tools—Speech
Price's List of Lists	gwis2.circ.gwu.edu/~gprice/listof.htm	Web-List
Privada.net	www.privada.net	Anonymous
Private Equity Network	www.nvst.com/	Mergers & acquisitions
ProFusion	www.profusion.com	Search tools
Publist	www.publist.com	Business cases/publications
Quicken	www.quicken.com	Company information
Real Time Stock Quotes	www.freerealtime.com	Stock quotes
Recap Signals-Biotech Industry Analsys	www.recap.com/	Industry
Redherring Magazine	www.redherring.com	News & magazines
Reference	www.reference.com	Discussion
Reference Library of Standards Organizations	web.ansi.org/public/library/internet/resources.html	Directory
Research Firms—Links	www.isoc.org/internet/stats/	Links
Round Zero	www.roundzero.com	Forum
San Jose State Library	www.library.sjsu.edu/	Library-General
SavvySearch	www.savysearch.com	Search tools
SCIP.org	www.scip.org/	Competitive Intelligence
Search Engine Watch	www.searchenginewatch.com	Web-Update
Search Tools & Directories	gwis2.circ.gwu.edu/~gprice/direct.html	Directory
Seed Stage.com	www.seedstage.com	Startups
Semi-Electronic Links	www.analog.com/new/hotlist.html	Electronics Links
Silicon Valley Association of Software Entrepreneurs	www.svase.org	Software research

Silicon Valley Bank Entrepreneurs	www.thecapitalnetwork	Bank
SiliconValley.com	www.mercurycenter.com/svtech/reports/index.shtml	Silicon Valley News
SimbaNet	www.simbanet.com	Web
Simpli	www.simpli.com	Search tools
Small Business Knowledge Base	www.bizmove.com	Startups
smartmoney	www.smartmoney.com/marketmap.html	Market map
The Source for Lists on the Web	www.statejobs.com/list.html	Directory
SPYONIT	www.spyonit.com/Home	Web-Alert
Standard & Poor's Industry Surveys	[hardcopy]	Associations-"Top"
Standard Industrial Classification Search	www.osha.gov/oshstats/sicser.html	SIC
stats.bls.gov	www.stats.bls.gov	Government/statistics
stat-usa.gov	www.stat-usa.gov	Government/statistics
Technology Evaluation	www.technologyevaluation.com	Research on IT spectrum
techweb	www.techweb.com	News & magazines
Telco Exchange	www.telcoexchange.com/	Industry-Telecom
Telecom Industry Organizations Links	www.sonoma-systems.com/resources/industry-links.html	Industry-Telecom
Telecom Information Resources (Michigan)	china.si.umich.edu/telecom/associations.html	Industry-Telecom
Telecommunications Industry Association	www.tiaonline.org/	Industry-Telecom
Telecommunications Magazine Online	www.telecommagazine.com/	Industry-Telecom
Telecommunications Reports International	www.tr.com/	Industry-Telecom

(continues)

Source Name	Location	Type
Telecoms Virtual Library	www.analysys.com/vlib/	Industry-Telecom
Tenkwizard	www.tenkwizard.com	SEC filings
Top 20 Business Links	www.ziplink.net/top20.html	Business Links
Totalnews	www.totalnews.com	General news
Towergroup	www.towergroup.com	Market research
Trade Association Network Challenge	www.brainstorm.co.uk/TANC/Directory/TA-ALL.html	International-(UK) associations
Trade Association Research (Research Bank Web)	www.investex.com	Analysis
Ulrich's International Periodicals Directory	Dialog- /Nexis	Publications directory
United States Telephone Association	www.usta.org	Industry-Telecom
University of North Carolina at Charlotte	www.uncc.edu/lis/referencelintbus/vibehome.htm	Library-Business
Upside	www.upside.com	News & magazines
US Commerce's International Trade Administration	www.ita.doc.gov/ita_home/itakeyin.html	International
US Industry & Trade Outlook	www.ntis.gov	Industry
US Private Companies	www.rmonline.com/armusa.htm	Company (Private)
VentureOne	www.ventureone.com	Company (Venture capital)
Vertical Net	www.verticalnet.com	Trade communities
Vista Information Solutions	www.vistainfo.com	Business
Webmate	www.webmate.com	Search tools
Webopaedia	www.webopaedia.com	Technology reference
WebSeeker	www.bluesquirrel.com	Search tools
WEFA Reports	www.wefa.com	Market research reports

whatis	www.whatis.com	Technology reference
wired	www.wired.com	News & magazines
Wireless LAN	www.wlana.com	Industry-Telecom
WirelessNOW	www.wirelessnow.com/newlinks.lasso	Industry-Telecom
Working Press of the Nation	Nexis-	News
WorldVest Base	www.wvb.com	International Companies
WOW-COM Consumer Resource	www.wow-com/consumer/	Industry-Telecom
WSRN-Market Cap	www.wsrn.com/home/dataset/search.html	Financial Information
XLS	www.xls.com	Financial
Yahoo	www.yahoo.com	Search tools
Yankee Group	www.yankeegroup.com/webfolder/yg21a.nsf/Pages/home	IT Research
ZDNet	www.zdnet.com	IT Research
Zero Knowledge Systems	www.freedom.net	Anonymous
Ziplip	www.ziplip.com	Anonymous
Zoomerang	www.zoomerang.com	Surveys

Index

Index

Index

Index

Index

DATE DUE

JAN 2 2010